Travels in a Tree House

Also by John S. Workman

Fireflies in a Fruit Jar
Open Windows

Travels in a Tree House

John S. Workman

Essays on Life and Other Joys

From the Pen of an Arkansas Minister/Journalist

Being a Collection of Essays Published in the Arkansas Gazette
and the Arkansas Democrat–Gazette between the Years 1989
and 1992, and with One Chapter of Previously Unpublished
Essays

The University of Arkansas Press
Fayetteville
2001

Copyright © 2001 by The University of Arkansas Press

All rights reserved
Manufactured in Canada

05 04 03 02 01   5 4 3 2 1

Designer: John Coghlan

⊗ The paper used in this publication meets the minimum requirements of the American National Standard for Permanence of Paper for Printed Library Materials Z39.48-1984.

The columns previously published in the *Arkansas Gazette* and the *Arkansas Democrat-Gazette* are used with permission, © *Arkansas Democrat-Gazette,* 2001.

Library of Congress Cataloging-in-Publication Data
Workman, John S., 1927–
  Travels in a tree house : essays on life and other joys / John S. Workman.
     p. cm.
A collection of essays published in the Arkansas gazette and the Arkansas Democrat-gazette between the 1989 and 1992, and with one chapter of previously unpublished essays.
  ISBN 1-55728-705-8 (pbk. : alk. paper)
  1. Meditations. 2. Workman, John S., 1927– I. Arkansas gazette. II. Arkansas Democrat-gazette. III. Title.
  BV4832.3 .W67 2001
  242—dc21
                                                              2001000368

To our grandchildren
John Thomas, Jennifer, Julia, Marcus, Harrison, Phoebe, and Joshua

My heart is light with the friends I make,
And better friends I'll not be knowing;
Yet there isn't a train I wouldn't take,
No matter where it's going.
                    —Edna St. Vincent Millay (1921)

Contents

XI
Other Journeys

XII
Up, Up, and Away
Through the Valley of the Sun

Foreword

So many have said it: Life is a journey. A voyage. A venture. Life—at times a pleasant stroll, at times a storm-tossed passage, at times perhaps even a pilgrimage. But always life is journey. Always life is adventure.

Whatever words may be employed to characterize its marvel and mystery, life is movement. From first moment to last breath, to live is to move. To live is to travel, to saunter, to run. To live is to grow, to change. To live is to know both joy and sorrow, pain and pleasure. To live is to slip—perhaps even to slide, glide, stumble, or be pushed against all resistance—finally into death itself. From start to finish, from cradle to grave, to live is to move on.

It is with such a perception—journey as metaphor for life—that these collected essays are offered. But let the reader be informed: This is not a "travel book" in the usual sense. Although there is a smattering of that sort of activity herein—accounts of movement across bits of geography—such is not the collection's principal focus.

Herein, rather, are accounts of inner journeys, wanderings across the map of the mind, travels within the heart. And, yes, even a presumptuous expedition or two along the frontier of that mystical realm called spirit. And all this couched as comment upon happenings of the day, happenings during specific moments in time, in specific places as expressed by a specific traveler.

A reminder: This is "a collection," a gathering of separate, mostly unrelated essays written across a span of years. Here is not a novel with a plot; or a narrative with a story to tell; or a treatise with a single point to make. "What, then," the reader might ask, "is this book all about? What is this collection's unifying theme?"

It is about life, and the journey through life—a unifying theme that is progressively reflected in each succeeding chapter title. And just as life so often resists organization into neat categories—life is filled with surprise, mystery, and even chaos—so the placement of these essays within specific chapters is often rather capricious. Such placements have been made because the essay in question "just seems to fit best" under a particular chapter heading.

It occurs that something of a similar agony to "explain" his work was experienced by Mark Twain, who handled his problem quite convincingly by placing the following in the introductory pages of *The Adventures of Huckleberry Finn:*

Notice
Persons attempting to find a motive in this narrative will be prosecuted; persons attempting to find a moral in it will be banished; persons attempting to find a plot in it will be shot.

So herewith—and without the fear of being prosecuted, banished, or shot!—is a traveler's kit bag stuffed with a variety of snacks for trekkers along life's trail. Some of these offerings might be sweets, others more nourishing fare, and, with the blessing, not too many will be tossed as junk food. In any event, all are served with the hope that life's surprise, mystery, joy, and other grand gifts might greet each traveler who happens this way.

All but one of the essays in chapters 1 through 11 originally appeared as columns of opinion on the religion pages of the *Arkansas Gazette,* where I was religion editor and columnist for twelve years until that paper's demise in October 1991, and in the *Arkansas Democrat-Gazette,* where I was a religion columnist for one year. Chapter 6 is an expanded version of a feature article that appeared in the *Arkansas Democrat-Gazette.*

Minor editorial changes (principally for paragraph structure and length) have been made in some of the columns as they were originally published. Appreciation is expressed to the *Arkansas Democrat-Gazette* for permission to reproduce these writings in this collection.

As noted at the beginning of chapter 12, the essays therein were written after my retirement and have not been previously published.

John S. Workman
Conway, Arkansas
Winter 2000

CHAPTER I

Of Daydreams and Journeys

Dreaming men are haunted men.
—Stephen Vincent Benet (1928)

1

After All, It Was Only a Tree House

Mark the date: Thursday, September 27, 1990. The end of an era. No, it didn't make the history books nor lead the evening news. Earth didn't shake nor heaven tremble. Nor could you be expected to care a whole lot about any of this. After all, it was only a tree house.

That Thursday, a week before this writing, my wife and a friend and I dismantled our tree house at our family cabin on Magazine Mountain. After a quarter century of good times, our tree house, now bested by the elements and a danger to curious climbers, had to go. Although most of its wood was of no further use, we didn't just "tear down" our tree house. We dismantled it, with due respect, and even a bit of ceremony.

On this morning several days later, scrapbook in hand, I reviewed the photos, browning with age, that tell the story of how, with our four children, we built our tree house. We dreamed its shape, drew its plans, cut its pine poles and skinned off their bark. We built our platform in the sky without a single nail or bit of metal violating the host tree, a grand century-old white oak.

Decades ago, the old tree had lost its top, most probably during a windstorm. With its two remaining arms uplifted, the noble oak had long begged for a tree house. For twenty and more summers our tree-top platform served well.

From our tower in the sky we had a breathtaking view overlooking the Petit Jean River valley, some one thousand feet below. We could enjoy an unobstructed view of sixty miles or more toward the west, south, and east. A scant three miles to the northwest, Magazine Mountain's majestic brow loomed above us, an ever-present teacher of one of life's vital lessons: To succeed in the Eternal Quest—to glimpse Truth, Beauty, Majesty, and Grace—one must not only look forward, down, and behind; one must also look up. One must look Above.

From our skyseat one could greet the morning, hot chocolate in hand, and watch clouds uncover valleys and mountain ranges in the distance. Here one could watch the sun rise and set. And watch storms build and die in the distance. Or, perhaps, one could, from this lofty perch, be chased by sudden storms to shelter in the cabin below, to enjoy the warmth from the friendly fireplace.

On our sky platform, beneath sun, moon, and Milky Way, one could play all sorts of children's games. Here one could sleep under a sky so heavy with stars their weight could be felt. Here one could watch buzzards soar from one county to the next. And, through binoculars, one could watch the little crop duster airplane skirt the east end of the mountain and float down between Big Snake and Little Snake Knobs as it dusted crops in the valley far, far below.

Here one could read, or dream, or think. Or, better still, do nothing. And from this launching pad in the sky, one could venture on journeys to distant times and faraway places. From here, one could travel. From here, one could travel in a tree house.

It was quite a creation, even if I say so myself. My tree house just may have been the eighth best thing I've ever done in my entire life.

At one point in last week's dismantling my wife said it: "I hope all this won't be too difficult for you." It was a tender thing to say, exactly the right thing to say. But, truth to tell, there was more a feeling of celebration than grief, though something like grief was there. I thought of a story that a minister friend told at a funeral. About an old tree trimmer who was asked how he managed to swing so fearlessly from limb to limb, high above the ground, supported only by a thin rope.

"You have to learn how to turn loose without letting go," the old man said. It's a good lesson for life, useful even in saying farewell to a tree house. There comes a time when we all have to turn loose. But we don't have to let go.

—*Arkansas Gazette,* October 6, 1990 (revised and adapted).

2

Clouds from Both Sides

Somewhere on a distant airstrip the Red Baron taxies his open-cockpit biplane toward the runway.

Something is different this morning. The brisk autumn air carries a sharper chill than usual. The fearless flying ace pulls his greatcoat closer around him, ties his scarf, tightens his helmet, and adjusts his goggles.

Before starting his dash down the runway he pauses a moment. An eternity. Yes, something is different. Something one can feel but can't comprehend. A shiver one can't shake with the morning fog. . . .

High over Faulkner County, Arkansas, the trim little blue-and-white Beechcraft floats lazily over the lovely green countryside. The takeoff, moments earlier from Conway, was directly into a blazing sunset. Marvelous!

"Great flying weather," the ace instructor says to the excited young dreamer in the right-hand seat. "Yeah, great," Young Dreamer shouts back, perhaps louder than necessary, forgetting for a moment that this is a closed-in cabin. No open cockpit here, no helmets, no scarves (shucks), and no need to shout. At least not out loud.

Young Dreamer bides his time, letting Ace Instructor keep the controls as long as it pleases him. Soon it happens. "Okay, now what you do if you want to turn to the left is move this wheel this way. And if you want to turn right, move it that way. And these foot things—you press on these if you want to bank as you turn."

The lesson took twenty seconds. (Naturally, Young Dreamer didn't really need it, since he'd been doing this, in his head, regularly since his first airplane ride more than a half century earlier, when he was about nine years old.)

Young Dreamer takes the controls. Crowded among all those other thoughts racing through his being, it came: "Wherever the Red Baron is this evening, that rascal won't sleep well tonight!"

Evil now is doomed. Righteousness will, at long last, prevail.

The good guys are going to win. Somewhere amid a great cloud of witnesses, John Wayne joins Moses, Marco Polo, and John Wesley in rooting Young Dreamer on. "Go, Johnny, go! You can do it!"

"Am I doing anything that'll get you in trouble with the Feds," Young Dreamer, ever the moral man, asks. Ace Instructor replies: "We're not doing a thing that's illegal. Keep at it." Since Ace Instructor comes from a fine Presbyterian family and goes to Sunday school at the Methodist Church, that's good enough for Young Dreamer.

"What I'm going to do," Young Dreamer informs Ace Instructor, "is make a few S turns. Get ready."

"Now I'm going to turn to the right and bank sharply. Hang on!" Another successful maneuver. Ace Instructor remains remarkably calm.

"That's Petit Jean Mountain over there," Ace Instructor is saying. "And that's Nebo, and way over yonder is Magazine Mountain."

Young Dreamer announces his flight plan: "I'm going to take us around the edge of Morrilton, over by Overcup Lake and Beaver Lake and then we'll fly the Hump (a two-hundred-foot ridge just north of Conway) and head back to the field."

The unimaginative will call this "just another airplane ride." Don't you believe it. And don't try to tell the Red Baron that that's all it was.

—*Arkansas Gazette*, October 28, 1989.

3

In Search of Life's Meaning Aboard *Starship*

When this newspaper hits your doorstep, I'll be bouncin' around in a Chevy van playing highway games with a couple of our grandchildren. We'll be on a vacation trip to New York State. Our mission: To give official and proper welcome to the newest member of our extended family, another grandchild, our fourth. You didn't ask to hear about all this, but here goes. (I'm out of state, safely away from the phone.)

This is written a couple of days before our June 24 departure. In addition to welcoming Marcus, second child of our son John and daughter-in-law Andrea, what this is gonna be is a camping trip.

Aboard the van *(Starship Enterprise Jr.)*, which will be pulling a popup camp trailer *(Slumber Module One)*, will be our next-to-oldest son, Steve (mission commander); his children and our grandchildren—John Thomas, age eleven (first officer), and Jennifer, age nine, (real first officer). Also bounding along will be my wife (mission specialist one) and myself (mission specialist thirteen).

Steve's wife, our daughter-in-law Kathy (base control), a newly named school principal, will be attending university classes and will have to miss this high adventure. (Kathy, smartest of the bunch, chose to enroll in graduate school rather than spend twelve days and a couple of thousand or more miles in a six-by-ten-foot metal box hurtling cross-country in the July heat. I can understand why she's been chosen for high office.)

As I write this, our trip is viewed from the "anticipation" phase. As you read this, we'll be in the "realization" phase—actually en route. Then, in a few days from now, we'll come to phase three, the "reflection" phase. I must confess that I really don't know which phase is best.

Anticipation, with all the fun of planning, list making, map reading, campsite securing, etc., has its own special joys. So, too, does the realization phase, which by all rights should be the best of the three. This is when you're in the midst of the experience—when the concrete ribbon unfolds new vistas around every bend; when summer scenes of mountains, lakes, and towering clouds bring joy to the heart.

This current phase, realization, is when good company and campfire meals and starry nights make glad the soul. This is when sleeping beneath the stars invites the mind to travel to lands away and worlds unknown. Marvelous.

And then, at the end of the trail, after *Starship* has been parked in the carport and the borrowed camper returned to its generous owners—then comes the sweetness of reflection.

Ah, reflection. Yet one more grand series of experiences to tuck away securely in the storehouse of memory. There, safe so long as the mind cooperates, are grand memories, ready for recall on long winter nights when storms rage and sleep stays awake.

Such experiences—anticipation, actualization, and reflection—remind us that life is whole, that it is all of a piece. And that life is grand!

Okay, I've told you about my vacation. Now it's your turn. Only don't bring the photos.

—*Arkansas Gazette,* July 1, 1989.

4

The Whole Truth About Freedom

I've got it right here on my desk, this cartoon. This cartoon on this postcard sent to me by my brother. My brother who lives in Houston. The one in Texas.

Only he sent the postcard from Colorado, my brother did, while on vacation. He's sort of a Republican, my brother is, and a lawyer to boot, although that doesn't have anything to do with this cartoon. (I suppose he's still a Republican, my brother, and I suppose he's still a lawyer, although after all that went on in Houston this week—that Republican National Convention—I'd understand if he's decided to repent of both conditions.)

But whatever, all that has nothing at all to do with this cartoon. The cartoon shows a motorcycle broken down alongside a lonely deserted road. The rider is nowhere to be seen, nary a living thing is in sight. The motorcycle's rear wheel has been removed, and nuts, bolts, and wrenches are scattered about. One can visualize the now-enraged rider toting or rolling the heavy wheel miles toward civilization to have it repaired.

Just behind the disabled vehicle is a cycle camping trailer, indicating that this stalwart adventurer was headed for an exciting vacation in the wilds. Away at last, liberated from the hassles, frustrations, constraints, and problems of civilization!

Across the back of the trailer, in bold letters, is the single word: "Freedom!"

Ah yes, freedom.

Ah, yes, to be free from interruptions; to be liberated from worries; to be released from responsibilities; to be done with pesky chores; to break the shackles of duty that mess up one's personal agenda.

Ah, yes, to be free! Who among us has not felt the stirrings? Who has not known the longing?

Having done a bit of motorcycle camping myself, and having endured sufficient roadside repairs, I can identify with this cartoon, which now I keep before me as a reminder of a fundamental truth: Freedom, at least as it is popularly perceived, isn't nearly as free as it's cracked up to be. Freedom, at least as we fantasize it, has a hard time living up to its reputation. Freedom doesn't necessarily mean what we've been told it means.

To put it bluntly, freedom—the popularized version, anyway—isn't really all that great. Somebody along the way didn't tell us the whole truth about freedom.

The biblical religions long have known the real truth about freedom. They posit freedom not so much as self-centered liberty and license but rather as a matured sense of responsibility. Freedom, rather than license to do as one pleases, is more an open door to something called servanthood.

That, admittedly, is a concept that a self-centered, pleasure-seeking generation finds difficult to understand, much less admire and pursue. Early people of faith spoke of "bondage" to their Lord—lived out in service to others—as being the way to perfect freedom.

Last week my wife and I and a group of friends went to a dinner theater to see *Big River*, that delightful musical adaptation of Mark Twain's *Adventures of Huckleberry Finn*. At one point, young Huck asks a poignant question of Jim, the runaway slave who dreams of freedom. "What are you going to do with your freedom, Jim?"

It's a question always at the heart of the biblical concept of freedom. It's a question for the individual. It's a question for any nation that makes much of the value of freedom. What are we going to do with our freedom? Perhaps that's not an inappropriate question to ponder on a Saturday morning.

—*Arkansas Democrat-Gazette*, August 22, 1992.

5

This Man Actually Talks to His Bicycle

What you need to do right now is to lay aside this newspaper, jump into your pickup, and drive over here to my house and take a look at this bicycle. You won't believe it unless you see it.

Why, it's Old Jim!

Old Jim, my ten-speed bike and faithful friend of many a mile on the open road. Old Jim, for whom I paid twenty-five dollars, secondhand, almost fifteen years ago. Old Jim, who during those years has logged no less than fourteen thousand miles, count 'em, touring and camping throughout the Arkansas outback.

Old Jim, upon whose memory is etched such gems as sunsets from atop Rich Mountain, grueling ascents of the perilous east face of Petit Jean (no less than four times, at least), and the exhilaration of near-speed-limit, or so it seemed, dashes along Delta rice fields, hurled onward by a stout following wind. And—dare we recall it?—the challenge of Magazine Mountain in August!

You've come a long way, Old Jim. And to think that we both thought, silly us, that you wanted to rest for a spell. We really didn't believe it then, and we certainly don't believe it now. Yes, Jim, your restlessness has been showing, even through all that road grit and the dust of this junky garage storeroom. You know it and I know it: There are still grand adventures, noble escapades in your rusty old bones.

And so it was that about a month ago I at last got started on a long-dreamed-of project. I'd restore Old Jim. Completely. From stem to stern. Top to bottom. And—the part Jim was to like best— I'd scrape off all that old brown paint and rust and remove those road marks. And I'd slap on a whole new set of clothes.

"Sun Yellow" it said on the spray-paint can, a bargain at ninety-nine cents. And what a neat name, Sun Yellow. Jim likes the sun, and yellow is fitting for spring. And, yes, the color is appropriate for this Lenten and Easter season, too. And that's nice, you see, because Jim is pretty religious, for a bicycle.

Old Jim. Redeemed. Converted. Given new life. A fresh beginning. Resurrected, you might say. Old Jim born again.

So now, just this week, here's Old Jim—new paint job completed, several worn-out parts replaced, rust completely removed, and his whole bony being resplendent in Sun Yellow. And that old chrome, thought to be beyond restoration, now glistening brightly! Old Jim reborn. Glory hallelujah.

Okay, John—that's Old Jim talking now—it's your turn now. Come on. It's Lent and it'll soon be Easter. Get with the program. You need to get scrubbed up, too. You need to get, you know, reborn.

Actually I'd thought a bit about that myself. Quite a bit, in fact. I do so, from time to time. Think about getting reborn. Again. But getting reborn is a pretty tough deal. I remember what Jimmy Carter's brother Billy said when asked if he'd "experienced the second birth," if he'd been reborn. "Why," he said, "I haven't hardly gotten over being born the first time."

In truth, this mystery of spiritual renewal is surely one of the grand and glorious gifts of the Creator. Whatever words one might use to describe it, and within whatever religious tradition, the mystery and miracle of spiritual renewal is one of the all-time great gifts of the Great Gifter.

But unlike old bicycles, rebirth for us humans is, in my opinion and experience, sort of a continuous and continuing project. We're always under construction. We're always in the process of being reborn. And the results can be truly something to behold. The Creator can scrub us up and make us look even better than Old Jim restored. And that, believe you me, is really saying something.

—*Arkansas Democrat-Gazette,* March 21, 1992.

6

Egad! Pleasure and Romance, Too!

I said I'd never do it, but I did. I surrendered. I have joined the consumer generation. (But at least I put up a good fight, for years.)

It happened Monday morning at the Piggley Wiggly food store, where I'd parked my bicycle and gone inside to shop. In what was a totally premeditated and planned decision, I purchased a can of coffee based solely on the promotional message on the can. Although I'd purchased the brand once before, when my regular economy coffee wasn't available, it was that message, inscribed oh so marvelously on the back of the can, that won me over.

Naturally, I had kept the can from my earlier purchase (never throw away a coffee can) and now, these several months later, during an idle moment when admiring the can's simple beauty, I chanced to read the message on the back. That did it. I scarce could wait the long night through, so eager was I to get to the store, plop down my $2.48, and hurry home to savor my treasure.

I can hear your questions: What in the world was on that can? What sort of advertising gimmick would convince such a hard-headed skeptic? Here's a glimpse of that message. I was informed that the coffee in that can was prepared especially for me—yes, for me—to give me "all the flavor of coffee sipped at a Parisian café alongside the Seine."

Ah, Paris! Ah, cafes alongside the Seine. Ah, sipping!

Resist all that, if you can. There was even a small cameo painting, a French Impressionist-style scene showing elegant people dining at a quaint outdoor café in a place that just had to be Paris. And I don't mean the one in Logan County.

If your heart is still not fluttering and your taste buds not watering, there's more. This very coffee, I was informed, was carefully blended by coffee connoisseurs, the way the French do it, for "a full-bodied coffee that is filled with pleasure and romance." Oh my stars. Pleasure and romance, no less.

Now we've got Paris, an outdoor café alongside the Seine, full-bodied flavor, and—pardon me—pleasure and romance! In advertising lingo this is called playing hardball. And all these years I'd thought I'd just been drinking a cup of coffee, and an economy brand at that. Is it any wonder I was won over?

But quickly now, let's get to the Sunday school lesson. Without intending any offense to the coffee people, the fact is that life, all by itself and without the aid of natural or artificial stimulants, has always offered some pretty abundant and generous blessings, including even—egad!—pleasure and romance. These and much, much more are part of the package.

Yes, there are those other things, too—pain, suffering, sorrow, ordinary humdrum days, and so on. Those, too, are part of the package. But perhaps it takes all these varied ingredients, a rich full-bodied blend, if you please, to enable us to savor fully life's truly wonderful blessings.

—*Arkansas Gazette,* May 12, 1990.

7

Of Magic Carpets and Escape Machines

As you read this, my wife and I will be in New York, visiting our oldest son and daughter-in-law and their two children and hearing our youngest son sing in an opera. We'll be seeing the big city and you won't.

There's something else I've been doing that I'll bet you haven't. I've been building an airplane and a car. That's right. The airplane, the plans for which emerged from my rather voluminous fantasy library, looks remarkably like a vantage Gypsy Moth, which antique plane buffs will remember as a dandy little open-cockpit biplane. The car is modeled after the twenty-year-old Volkswagen Beetle I used to own and still drive in my dreams.

Oh—did I mention that the airplane is about eight inches long and has a wingspan of about nine inches? And that the car is about six inches long and almost three inches high? The items, made from wood scraps carefully selected from the pile in my shop, are gifts for our grandchildren.

The plane, painted a dandy blue, yellow, and red, with a little wooden propeller that spins around when you blow on it, is for Julia, age three and a half. The car, blue like Grandpa's old VW Bug, is for Marcus, age nine months. (When Marcus gets old enough to fly, like his big sister, there'll be a plane for him, too.)

If Julia and Marcus have half as much fun playing with these toys as Grandpa did in building them, it'll be unbearable. Henry David Thoreau said it, or something like it: The joys of construction should not be reserved only for the carpenter. Old adventurers need to build toy airplanes every once in a while just to keep their hand in. And to keep their heart aloft.

As I sketched the plans for my little plane and car and fashioned their parts with saw, knife, sandpaper, and paintbrushes, I imagined the stories I'd tell my grandchildren. Yes, and without apology, these would be magic carpets, escape machines primarily for fun; vehicles to launch flights of fancy, adventures for young hearts, journeys for young souls.

But here also would be vehicles with an equally important function—to give growth and nourishment to young spirits. Here would be passage to faraway places with strange-sounding names. Here one could break the surly bonds of Earth and venture where no human had gone before. Here the mind could be stretched, the vision challenged, the soul enriched and the heart made glad.

Nor would these vessels shield their young riders from life's more harsh realities. In due time, when little travelers are road-wise and ready, these trusty crafts may become symbols of love and security that can help weather life's storms, however severe.

How grand to book passage on flights of fancy! How grand to dream, to wonder, to plan, to venture, to risk, to see clouds from both sides, and to discover what's around the next bend in the road. And how grand to travel with those you love, and who love you.

Get ready, Julia. The Gypsy is on the tarmac and the motor is idling. Yes, you can be the pilot. Get set, Marcus. The little "bug" is packed. The camping gear is aboard, the gas tank's full, and there's air in the tires. Yes, you get to drive!

—*Arkansas Gazette,* February 24, 1990.

CHAPTER II

Travel Companions

We do not mind our not arriving anywhere
nearly so much as our not having any company
on the way.
—*Frank Moore Colby (1921)*

1

Unlonesome Dove

It occurred to us the other evening, deep into the third quarter of TV's super-long miniseries *Lonesome Dove,* that the Holy Spirit surely must be exhausted by now.

Lordy, what sufferings we humans have inflicted—and what nobility we have exhibited—in our sometimes inhumane, sometimes heroic travelings through this barren land. The *Lonesome Dove* story, about an aging cowhand's last cattle drive, gives poignant and often horrifying and humbling glimpses into humanity's worst and best sides.

And to think that throughout the whole human venture, at least according to a well-tested religious belief, the Holy Spirit is among the travelers. Yes, the Holy Spirit, heaven's dove, is always among the sojourners along life's highways and byways, however uncertain the journey may be.

Though often ignored and frequently underrated, this Holy Spirit character is always present, if behind the scenes. This Traveler is on duty twenty-four hours daily, present everywhere with all the Creator's beleaguered vagabonds. Surely the Holy Spirit, with all that company, must be the most unlonesome dove of all.

The TV drama, though not an avowedly religious tale, is not without its reminders of how this Unlonesome Dove theory works. Grace's messengers—life's heavenly doves—most frequently come disguised as people. And sometimes as the most unlikely people. Some of the most ordinary and ornery among us can be the most authentic and most effective grace givers.

None of the earthy characters portrayed in *Lonesome Dove* would take kindly to being called religious. Far from it. This is a rough, tumbled, foul-mouthed, womanizing, and rascally bunch of horse and cattle thieves who, when their own interests are threatened, don't hesitate to render frontier justice on the spot. Yet this is also a bunch of ordinary humans, dreamers of dreams, doers of good deeds, lovers of life and family and friends.

And, yes, the work of the Unlonesome Dove is seen in their midst, as in flashes of gentleness and humanity and fundamental morality, however unrefined. Such moments reflect grandly on the human species. Even the most unlikely among us can be instruments of grace, however unwittingly. If that bothers you, blame it on the Creator.

So know this as you continue your wanderings down life's dusty and perilous trail: The Unlonesome Dove, the Creator's abiding presence, is with you, and may meet or confront or challenge or comfort you at any moment. And that encounter may occur in the next person you meet, however unlikely that prospect may appear.

Yes, that's a scary thought. But it's a comforting one, too.

Vaya con Dios, amigos. The Unlonesome Dove travels among us. Take heart.

—*Arkansas Gazette*, February 11, 1989.

2

What This World Needs Is a Good Reunion

Up until this year I could count on the fingers of one hand the number of reunions I've attended during my lifetime. But this year I've already been to three. And by next week, when about forty of my in-laws gather at our house for Thanksgiving, the total will climb to four.

And after that there'll still be five weeks left in 1990, and it's frightening to contemplate how many reunions one could squeeze into five weeks if one tried really hard. It boggles the mind. And it doesn't do much to settle the nerves, either.

It's presumptuous to assume that others might be interested in one's own reunion experiences. But indulge me a few moments while I report on the most recent reunion I attended. This reunion was special to me, and it occurred just this past weekend in Florida.

Present were thirty-seven people, the large majority of whom hadn't seen each other in some thirty to forty-five years. I, for one, had not seen a single person in the group since 1945. A common bond united the diverse group that met for three days last week on Captiva Island near Fort Myers: A love of sailing and an association with Wilmette Harbor, on Lake Michigan in Illinois, and the harbor's Sheridan Shore Yacht Club.

The gathering took me back to what seems an ancient incarnation. To the summers of my high school years when I worked at the harbor as a "dingy boy," rowing people from the dock to their boats (at twenty cents an hour, later raised to a quarter). Our family lived in Wilmette for eight years when my father worked with a Chicago-based agency of the Methodist Church.

How grand were those summers at the harbor! How wonderful the associations, how fun the sailing, how exciting to crew on the various sailboats during race season. And now, these forty-five years later, how strange it seems, in landlocked Arkansas, to speak of sailing, to remember those rough "nor'easters."

I confess that at first I wasn't especially eager to make this reunion trip. There was something about it that, well, frightened me. Perhaps you can understand that.

However, my wife encouraged me to go, and to make the trip alone. I warned her that it was entirely possible that when I was a teenager I was in love, or something like it, with about half the girls who would be at the reunion. A wise woman, she encouraged me to go anyway.

She was right, of course. It was a grand and wonderful experience.

Reunions serve a vital function. By affording an occasion to renew old friendships, share joys and sorrows and good times and bad, reunions enable us to say something we probably didn't really know how to say when we were young. That we do, in fact, love each other; that we were—and that we remain—so very important to each other, even though we now may live in different places and in different worlds.

Perhaps there's a larger lesson in reunions. Perhaps what this beleaguered and frightened world, so torn by division, really needs is a good reunion. Perhaps our most fundamental need is to touch base with our past, to find our moorings and thereby better chart our course through an uncertain future.

Reunions help us celebrate each other. They help us to be thankful. Surely our world could stand a bit more of that.

—*Arkansas Gazette,* November 17, 1990.

3

The Trouble with Harry and Other Joys

I thought of him again just the other day. Harry. I don't know Harry's family name. I don't believe I ever did. But I remember Harry, and I need to tell you about him.

Harry came to mind the other day during one of my evening bicycle rides in the neighborhood. I'd just passed a lovely home where a gardener, obviously a hired hand—an ethnic minority one doesn't see too often in that neighborhood—was tending a tidy lawn. I thought of Harry.

To tell you about Harry, I have to go way back into my past, back to my early teen years when our family lived in a suburb of Chicago. That was in the early forties, shortly after the beginning of World War II.

Those were years of widespread paranoia about Japanese people, even those who were U.S. citizens. Those were the years of the relocation camps, where Japanese citizens of this country were placed after being taken from their homes.

Enter Harry. That was the trouble with Harry. He was Japanese. Elderly. Alone.

I never fully understood how Harry happened to come into our lives, but as I recall, it was something like this: Unless Harry could find work and people who would vouch for him, he would have to go to one of those camps. And so Harry became our gardener, though we really didn't have a garden that merited the dignity of the name.

Harry tended what little flowers we had, did odd jobs around the house, and was an ever-present help with whatever might be the task at hand. Although my memory is hazy regarding many things about Harry, I do remember that he was a hard and tireless worker, meticulous in his care of the lawn, always kind and polite to the extreme, and took genuine interest in our family's various activities.

And I remember another thing: Our parents assumed no small risk by befriending Harry. Readers who remember those frightening post–Pearl Harbor days can appreciate the social pressures assumed by befriending a Japanese person.

There is another thing regarding Harry that I remember, and that quite vividly—my parents calling a family conference to tell my two brothers and me about Harry's having to leave, and why. Harry had to leave because another job—one, our parents told us, he had long sought—had finally opened for him.

Harry left to join the faculty of Northwestern University, where he was to teach. Harry, we learned, was in fact "Dr. Harry" somebody, a highly trained scientist, a specialist of no small reputation.

I've thought often of Harry, who surely must have long since passed. I think of Harry as I see the countless thousands of distressed and displaced persons throughout this world, persons who, though perhaps not skilled or highly trained, are of inestimable worth simply by the fact of their being.

The gifts Harry gave to me have proved imperishable. Friendship, devotion, dignity.

But perhaps the gifts I treasure most from our family's "Harry Years" are those that our parents, both now deceased, gave to us three sons. The gift of values. The gift of caring. The gift of loving. The gift of taking a risk for something that is right.

I think often of Harry. And even more often these days I remember, with great pride, parents who risked no small bit in order to do the right thing.

—*Arkansas Gazette,* August 31, 1991.

4

Right-Brained Man, Left-Brained Woman

I hesitate to ponder what would have become of me if I had married a right-brained woman. Lucky for me (I'm right-brained,

I'm told), I married a left-brained lady and it's been my salvation. My salvation second to my religion, that is. I'm still trusting grace to get me into that place where even a left-brained woman couldn't get me.

Actually, I don't know a lot about these right-brain left-brain theories. Only that we right-brainers are supposed to be artist types. Writers, musicians, sensitive people, that sort of thing. You know, geniuses.

Left-brainers are supposed to be a whole lot more practical. They're good at doing things like keeping checkbooks balanced, figuring out income tax forms, making correct change, that sort of thing. Practical, sense-making work is what left-brained people do best.

We right-brainers are less practical, less sensible, you might say. We do things like fiddle on computers for awhile and then go outside and piddle around—make doodads out of junk, clean up storerooms, fix our bicycles, mow our lawns, keep our birdfeeders full, and watch the seasons change.

When we right-brainers tire of doing these sorts of things, we turn to less important work, like trying to figure out ways to save the universe. Other than all this, we right-brainers don't have a whole lot to do, and that's just as it should be. We're special. We're national treasurers is what we are.

And, oh, yes. There's something else that left-brained spouses do. They keep their right-brained spouses out of jail, which is where we'd all be if such things as paying taxes, meeting bills, remembering important appointments, answering letters, and such were not done by our left-brained spouses.

It probably says so somewhere in the Bible, though I haven't come across it, that we human are supposed to marry across-brain. We're supposed to marry someone whose brain works on the other side than our own.

Anyway, be all this as it may, there's a point to these ponderings (which is another thing we right-brained people do; we try to figure out the point of things, like the meaning of life, that sort of thing). The point to these right-brained ponderings is this: We're all different, and that difference is a grand, wonderful, beautiful thing.

The Creator has made us all different. In fact, there are probably all sorts of "sides" to our brains—right, left, middle, front, back, top, bottom, and so on and on. And the differences are a marvelous thing indeed.

It's at this point where this business of religion comes in. As this right-brainer sees it, one of the functions of religion is to help society celebrate all of these many differences. No, our differences aren't always easy to tolerate. It's not easy, this living in a world where all of us are different. It's not only not easy, it's often downright next to impossible.

And, more often than we like to admit, our differences provoke conflict, as this weary planet's long history of wars will attest. So, enter religion. The wisdom of the ages. The insights of revelation. The wonders of grace. The miracles of love. The double-edged sword of justice. The power of redemption. The blessedness of mercy. The gift of reconciliation. The wonder of grace and peace.

Right-brain, left-brain, whatever. It's all the work of the Creator. It's all beautiful. It's all to be celebrated.

Now, if you'll excuse me, the right side of my brain has just told me it's time to go outside and sit in my rocking chair and contemplate the wonder, beauty, and mystery of this marvelous world.

—*Arkansas Democrat-Gazette*, June 27, 1992.

5

Of the Man, the Van, and the Dog

There they go again, that man and his dog. In their van. That man, that dog, that van. That tan van. (Actually, it's a white van, but that doesn't rhyme.)

That man and his dog in their tan van, driving north on Mitchell Street, past my front window. Just as they do every day or so of every week in the year. For the past several years. That man, his tan van, his dog. Or perhaps it's that dog, his tan van, his man.

From my vantage point through my study window, a measured

115 feet from the street, I can observe and conclude this much: This is a nice man, probably retired, a respected citizen. Distinguished. Probably a Methodist. The van is new, just several months old. I know this because I used to see this delightful duo drive by in a regular car, an older model. Then on one bright morning here they came in their sparkling new van! Their new tan van (only it's really white). Nice.

The dog, too, I can observe. He (or perhaps she) is not as new as the van, though he or she is certainly not old. Pert, well groomed, seemingly in good health. Obviously happy. Always sitting up straight in the passenger-side front seat. Ears alert. Observant. Taking it all in. Enjoying the ride. Smile on face. Perhaps a Unitarian.

Where are they going, this respectable man, this nice tan van, this happy dog? What is their mission? What are they up to, these three, on their almost-daily journeys? Perhaps, I've thought, they are going to visit the man's elderly sister, who is shut in at her home nearby, stove up with arthritis, down in her back, getting over a broken hip.

But if that's their destination, they take a curious route. Because sometimes at the corner just outside my window, the nice tan van turns to the right and sometimes it turns to the left. Perhaps this elderly sister moves around a lot. Probably not. That leaves another possibility. Perhaps it's the dog who's being taken to visit a friend. But that's not likely, you say.

That leaves yet another option, perhaps the more probable one in this mystery of the man, the tan van, and the dog: This pair and their van are simply out for their regular morning drive. A joy ride. Scoping out the neighborhood. Seeing the world. Checking to learn if all those lively young people have returned to the school across the street from our house. Nope. Not yet.

Any one of the above possibilities would be understandable. Everybody needs a mission. Everybody needs to help somebody. Everybody, even a dog, needs a friend to be with. Everybody needs to see the world. Everybody needs to have some joy.

But maybe I've got all of this wrong. Maybe this duo is just driving by my window to take a quick look at me, to check me out. I can hear it. The dog speaks: "There he is again, that funny-looking bald-headed fellow, still typing away on that silly machine and staring out at us. What a silly expression! Boy, I'll bet he wonders who we are. Sort of looks like he doesn't belong to anybody's church. Some fun! Bow wow."

Oh, well, even a dog—and maybe especially a dog—needs somebody to laugh at. But whatever, perhaps there's a parable in all this, some lesson about lives that touch others without ever crossing. About people (and other animals) we see though never meet, yet somehow know that our worlds are mysteriously intertwined. Some message about people we don't know, may never meet, yet people who nevertheless have a claim on us.

People like terrified orphans in Sarajevo. Multitudes starving in Somalia. Strangers unaware. Ships that pass in the night.

Have a good day, man, dog, and van. Enjoy your drive. And thanks for the silent reminder. Thanks for being there.

—*Arkansas Democrat-Gazette*, August 8, 1992.

6

"You're a Pretty Girl and You're All Mine"

Dadgum it, I did it again. Made another goof. Another of my far-too-many goofs. When will I ever learn?

It was one of those idle comments—a favorite breeding ground for goofs, I've learned—made during one of our evening strolls through the neighborhood, my wife and I. A glance to my left. Then, out of the blue: "You're a pretty girl and you're all mine."

My first hint was the silence. A bit longer than usual. Deafening. Oops, I'd done it again.

Liz: "I don't 'belong' to anybody."

I knew that, of course. Stupid me. When indeed am I ever going to learn? She was this way even long before this Year of the Woman in Politics. Her own person. I've always respected that. Been proud of it. Even liked it that way. The way it should be.

"You're all mine" is a pretty tacky thing—yes, a fundamentally erroneous, impertinent, paternalistic, and imperialistic thing—to say to another human being, most especially one's spouse. As though one should, or could, "own" one's spouse.

"You're all mine." As I recall, it was that sort of thinking, or at least that was one of the issues, that precipitated this country's longest and bloodiest war. About whether one human being should own another human being.

So mark up yet one more goof for John. But you need to hear this: I'm not totally to blame for this sort of thinking. You can blame Jo Stafford. Jo Stafford the vocalist of several decades past. And blame the whole mind-set of the forties and fifties, those lazy, hazy, crazy years that fashioned the thinking of those of us then in our formative years.

But back to Jo. Jo kept singing to me: "Watch the sunrise on a tropic isle, see the pyramids along the Nile; just remember, darling, all the while, you belong to me." There was more (Jo was sort of sweet on me): "See the marketplace in old Algiers, send me photographs and souvenirs; just remember, when a dream appears, you belong to me."

Jo wouldn't quit: "Fly the ocean in a silver plane, see the jungle when it's wet with rain; just remember, till you're home again, you belong to me."

Imagine! Pretty Jo Stafford (I never saw her, but I just knew she was pretty) was telling me that I belonged to her! How was I not to believe it, that I belonged to Jo? And that message, in my pre-enlightened years, sounded pretty okay to me.

So don't blame me if I still think in you-belong-to-me terms. It's hard to shake off the chains of the past.

As you might have guessed, there are larger dimensions to all this. Try this on: If you don't belong to another human being, then to what do you belong? What is it that possesses you?

Another singer used to complain that he was owned by the company store, to which he owed no less than his soul. For others of us, our "owners" have other names: The bank, the TV set, a habit, a hobby, a business. Sometimes I think I'm owned by my storeroom. It eats up all my time, my trying to keep it clean. It's as though I'm owned by the past.

Who owns us? It's an always-timely question, and it's a question to which the biblical religions speak. If I read their larger message correctly, these ancient faiths suggest that if one is to be owned, it's best to not be owned by things but by grand ideas, high ideals, inspiring visions, and by causes that are larger than ourselves.

The apostle Paul has a suggestion: "Behold, I show you a more excellent way." The way of love. Be owned by love, Paul suggests.

Yes, this is Saturday, and you deserve some rest. But put this in your head and think it: By whom, or by what, are you owned? By what special interests, by what causes, beliefs, and ideals are you possessed?

—*Arkansas Democrat-Gazette*, October 3, 1992.

7

I Think of Them Often, My Dolphins

I think of them often, my dolphins. Those frisky, high-leaping, fun-loving, beautiful dolphins. Those dolphins that cavorted so marvelously around our excursion boat last November off Captiva Island, Florida. Putting on a show, they were. A show especially for me and my thirty-six chums I hadn't seen for forty-five years.

And what a wonderfully appropriate treat, those dancing dolphins, at this reunion of old sailors. For we were dolphins all. And still are. Lovers of the sea. Adventurers. Old salts from way back, harbor rats from the Sheridan Shore Yacht Club and Wilmette Harbor (Illinois). A bunch of Lake Michigan deepwater sailors drawn together by tin-typed, wind-chimed memories of the way we were.

Dolphin memories. Splashing fun in the sea. Dolphin freedom. Dolphin wonder. Dolphin mystery. Dolphin joy.

There's a small detail—a minor one, really—regarding my Florida dolphins (the real ones that jumped around our excursion boat) that I suppose I ought to reveal: I never actually got to see them. That's right. I never really caught sight of those dolphins! As the frolicky creatures were jumping almost within arm's reach on one side of our vessel, to the joyous shouts and exclamations of our party, I was always on the other side of the boat.

By the time I'd rushed to the correct side, my dolphins were nowhere to be seen. They had, quite naturally and properly, hastened to the other side to entertain those of us there. The result: I never saw a single one of those marvelous creatures.

Woe is me. Story of my life. Always on the wrong side of the boat. "He never got to see the dolphins." Poor John. A fitting epitaph.

But whoa, hold on there. Truth to tell, I must confess that some of the most marvelous ventures I've ever enjoyed, some of the most profound truths I've ever experienced, have been those I have never actually seen with my eyes. You know the type of thing I'm talking about: Love. Joy. Inspiration. Faith. And so on.

And grand adventures. Ah yes, grand adventures.

I have, in fact, had a few truly grand adventures of the "real" kind, perhaps more than one could rightly expect. But I've had a generous quota of others, too—high adventures in that marvelous realm called imagination. And I'd have to admit that the latter are almost as sweet as the former.

Dolphins all, such adventures. Dolphins I've never seen, in fact, but nevertheless have enjoyed in my heart. It's true: The heart has treasures the eyes cannot surpass.

Such thoughts came to mind last week as I proudly showed a friend my patio restoration project. I'd designed what I called, for want of a better term, a "pagoda look" on the ends of a beam supporting our patio roof. My intention was to create a hint of oriental atmosphere.

My friend's comment: "If you ask me, it looks more like dolphins." (This is the same friend to whom some years ago I showed, also with great pride, a rocking horse I'd made for a grandchild. His comment then: "If you ask me, it looks more like a rocking sheep.")

But how wonderful, dolphins on my patio! How grand! Wooden dolphins to remind me daily of those special dolphins— all those marvelous wonders we may never actually see with our eyes but nevertheless may enjoy in our hearts.

Dolphin joy. It's a happy thought. A nice memory. A grand reality.

—*Arkansas Gazette,* April 27, 1991.

CHAPTER III

Seasons

Spring is never Spring unless it comes too soon.
—*G. K. Chesterton (1912)*

1

Turn Around and It's August

Sorry to have to break this news, but it's August already. In case you haven't noticed, today is the first day of a new month.

But where did July go? And June? Turn around and the months are gone. Turn around and it's August already. Before you know it.

Come next Saturday, there'll be only three weeks and a couple of days left in this new month. Then it'll be September! And before you realize it, October will be here and gone and, lo and behold, November will have slipped away and, wow, Christmas will be here! Before you know it.

Better start gathering firewood. Better start making Christmas lists. Christmas shopping right around the corner.

Why, just the other day we heard a fellow on the radio say something about a back-to-school sale. I live right across the street from a school and it seems only yesterday that classes let out for summer. Where does it all go, anyway, this stuff called time? My, my, my, how it slips away. Time.

Which raises a bunch of questions. Good August questions. When time slips away—or fades away, or passes, or whatever— where does it go? What happens to passed time?

Ah yes, August questions. Philosophical questions. Mind bogglers. Questions that make the brain sweat. Make it sore. Questions that make you wish you'd done something else, anything other than think. It ought to be against the law to think during August. Too hot.

August. A good month to put the brain in neutral. Almost as good as July. Let it idle. Spell words wrong. With or without an *e*.

But since this is only the first day in August, and since we didn't do much thinking in July anyway, maybe we could slip in just a tad of mental gymnastics. Not too much, mind you, just a bit. Like, for example, a few thoughts about this business of time.

What happens to time after it's spent? And what about "wasted" time, that sin we're all warned against? What happens to time that's "lost," to time that's ticked away, to time that's misused? Can one ever regain lost time? Time spent foolishly? Is there such a thing as reusing time? Can you recycle old time?

And where does all our used-up time go? Is it stored somewhere? Is there a time dump someplace? Maybe over in the next county?

I've got a theory: We humans used to be a whole lot more time conscious back in the good old days. Back when clocks and watches made noise, back when they actually ticked. I can remember that as a child all the clocks in our house—on our living room mantle, in the kitchen, in the bedrooms—ticked so loud you could hardly stand it.

Tick, tock; tick, tock; tick, tock. You could actually hear time passing and it made you nervous. You knew, without a doubt, that your life was running out, a tick and a tock at a time.

These days, when clocks don't tick or make any noise at all (except for those electronic wristwatch alarms that go off during the Sunday sermon), you don't even realize that time is expiring. "Burning daylight" is the way John Wayne used to put it.

Burning daylight. Using time. Moments, seconds, minutes, hours, days, months, years, all slipping away. Life slipping away. Gosh, that's sort of scary.

And here we are, we who are supposed to be bringers of good news, spreading all this gloom about life slipping away. You ought to be ashamed of yourself, wasting your time reading this sort of stuff.

It's August already. Put this paper down, this very minute, and go do something worthwhile. Maybe do a good deed. While there's still time.

—*Arkansas Democrat-Gazette*, August 1, 1992.

2

Three Cheers for God!

Okay, let's hear it for God: Hip, hip, hooray! Hip, hip, hooray! Hip, hip, hooray!

That's for this fall's breathtaking display of autumn colors, surely one of the most marvelous offerings in recent memory. At least that's been the case in our neighborhood. Magnificent!

But of course God always deserves cheers—and always more than the traditional three. But seldom more so than for autumn's beauty. How grand, how glorious, how inexpressibly splendid has been this fall's treat to the eyes. Indeed, the array has been a feast for the heart, a blessing to the soul.

Surely color is one of the Creator's most wondrous gifts. Reds, yellows, greens, maroons, oranges, crimsons, plumbs, chartreuses, browns, purples, rusts, mauves, lemons, umbers, limes, tomatoes, chocolates, and a whole array of other colors and mixtures the names for which I can't even imagine.

All these and more have been on brilliant and proud display as one walks the neighborhood.

My favorite would have to be the maples. It seems that even one single maple tree, at a particular stage in its turning, can have leaves of every imaginable color. Marvelous!

Light adds its own mysterious magic to the canvas. As beautiful as the trees are in sunlight, they are, in my opinion, even more splendid on cloudy days. Then it seems the leaves create their own light, an inner shining, a glowing, a warmth that one can almost feel. There's even a deliciousness, a sweetness, that one can almost taste. Something like strawberry or raspberry—or perhaps lime—sherbet. Picnic time in the Garden of Eden.

And yet how soon it all passes. A few days—even one brief day (sometimes even an hour or less) at the peak—and the magic begins to wane, the colors fade, the light dims, and the sugar looses its sweetness.

Perhaps it's best this way. Perhaps if it all were to last longer our hearts might explode, or maybe rupture or something like that, something not covered by insurance. Even Medicare. Perhaps if it were to last longer, even God couldn't stand it.

But wait. This, too—this briefness—is okay. What follows after the colors have gone also has its own specialness, its own grace, its own beauty. Winter, though less colorful, is not without its benedictions. Though stark and foreboding, the brown-leafed trees, soon to be bereft of their distinctive wardrobe, have their own dignity and loveliness, however harsh it may be.

Along my route this autumn I visit an old maple tree that is dying, not long for this world. I imagine it speaks:

Remember me as I am this autumn, in the days of my joy. Yes— think of me in spring, when I put on my new gown—but remember me best in my autumn splendor. This, really, is who I am. This, really, is what I have to say.

—*Arkansas Gazette*, November 10, 1990.

3

Lessons from Jim the Missionary

Back in my greener years, back when I knew a whole lot more than I know now, I used to think it was really neat how God had arranged the seasons to match the Christian calendar, the Christian year.

You know—how spring was to coincide with Lent, and how Advent and Christmas were to occur when there was lots of snow on the ground, just like it was in the Bible lands and just like Santa Clause and Bing Crosby intended it to be.

That was before I grew up, partly, and unlearned some things. And that was before my friend Jim, who had been a missionary in South America, finally became sufficiently tired of my associating Lent with spring and Christmas with snow and decided to educate me.

Jim the missionary, who had lived in the Southern Hemisphere, gently explained to me that down there the flowers bloom and the trees bud during what we in our Northern Hemisphere call fall, but which down there is actually spring. And that down there it snows during what we up here call summer, but which down there is in fact winter.

Don't tell me God doesn't have a sense of humor.

But anyway, Jim the missionary, being a sort of nice person, didn't exactly say that I was dumb. But he also didn't act as if that probability hadn't occurred to him. The long and short of it was that Jim the missionary messed up my mind. But I guess that's what missionaries are supposed to do.

So now, thanks to Jim the missionary, I've got a problem. Here it is Lent again, and about the only things I know to write about Lent are things that have mostly to do with spring. And since Jim the missionary is still hanging around, that, as we say in the Northern Hemisphere, "leaves me in a big quandary."

All of the above is to introduce a subject which, it seems to me, needs a whole lot more introducing than it gets during these days when so many world-class changes are taking place. That subject: The blessings—and curses—of cultural influence. More specifically, how "authentic biblical faith" (if we can be so presumptuous) is affected by the power of a culture's influence.

(Yes, this is a heavy subject for Saturday, but stay put in your pew. You need to think on this stuff.)

To a very large extent, we humans are products of the culture into which we were born. All of us have been birthed, nurtured, and molded within a particular culture—"the sea we swim in," as culture has been called.

This reality is both good and bad. Our cultural influences are a blessing to the extent they help us become more fully human, more loving, more committed to justice, more in partnership with the natural world. Those same cultural influences are a liability to the extent they hinder and limit such growth and development; to the extent they imprison us.

Now, concerning religion, the biblical faiths specifically: A too strong cultural influence produces a regional version of what is meant to be a universal faith. "American Christianity" is an example.

But why such a topic during Lent?

Because the whole Lenten season, which historically has been encumbered with a whole bunch of our Northern Hemisphere cultural influences—spring, bunny rabbits, and more—has messages that break the bars of cultural prisons. Lent's themes are universal: The yearning for spiritual connections and moorings, and the Creator's promise that such yearnings are being answered.

But such is just the tip of a very large subject. One wonders: How much "authentic biblical truth" are we insulated from because of our cultural prisons?

Prison-breaking takes a lot of letting go. And that takes a lot of trust. A lot of trust in God. A lot of trust in each other.

—*Arkansas Democrat-Gazette*, March 7, 1992.

4

The Wounded Bird: A Holy Week Parable

About a year ago, while fiddling around with words, I wrote the paragraphs printed below in italics. Although about a bird, the idea didn't fly. So I filed it away and forgot it.

Forgot it, that is, until a recent morning when an unexpected visitor appeared at my window. I'll pick up the story after this account of last year's fiddlings:

Off and on during the past few days I've been watching, through my study window, a wounded bird. Unable to fly, the little creature has been hobbling about, pecking the ground beneath my birdfeeder. Gleaning the fields, as it were.

The bird, apparently an adult, seems to have an injured left wing and leg. It flaps the affected wing and favors the leg, limping awkwardly and moving only with great effort.

I'm surprised that on this third day since first seeing my woe-stricken and grounded friend, that he—or she—is still alive. (I've decided, as much for sentiment as for style, to call my little friend a she.)

It is strange, the ways of nature: I find myself becoming quite attached to my new friend. Perhaps it's because we belong to the same fraternity. The fellowship of the wounded.

I should add that my friend is not very attractive. Just an ordinary bird—as I am just an ordinary man. This adventure might be more romantic, I suppose, if my friend were more a cardinal or a robin and I were more, say, a Robert Redford.

But no, she's just an ordinary, common bird. Wounded. Exposed to the dangers of a harsh and often unfriendly world.

I've thought what I might do to help my little friend. I suppose I could put her safely on a limb, out of harm's way. But then she couldn't forage. No risk, no prize. No pain, no gain.

What am I to do for this small creature? Surely I can't be expected to spend all my time standing guard over my little friend, now can I.

Can I?

Okay, we're back in the present now, a year later.

A few days ago, again at my desk, I noticed a lone bird at my feeder. Something about the little creature caught my eye. It hobbled as it moved. No, it jumped. On one leg! And its left wing drooped!

Immediately I searched my computer files and found "Wounded Bird." I opened those notes, studied my description of the bird seen a year ago, and became convinced that this bird now at my feeder must, in fact, be my long-lost wounded friend!

Unbelievable! Alive! Back home!

Just yesterday, while reading *Flight to Arras* by Antoine de Saint-Exupery, I happened upon a passage that seems hauntingly appropriate on this eve of Holy Week and during this week when, I do believe, I was granted a reunion with my wounded friend.

The book's author, then a pilot in the French airforce, tells of his emotions while watching the defeat of France early in World War II:

> Defeat. Victory. Terms I do not know what to make of. One victory exalts, another corrupts. One defeat kills, another brings life. Tell me what seed is lodged in your victory or your defeat, and I will tell you its future. Life is not definable by situations but by mutations. There is but one victory that I know is sure, and that is the victory that is lodged in the energy of the seed. Sow the seed in the wide black earth and already the seed is

victorious, though time must contribute to the triumph of the wheat.

Defeat. Victory. Energy of the seed. Thoughts aplenty for Holy Week.

—*Arkansas Gazette,* March 23, 1991.

5
True Confessions of a Great Lover

(Columnist's note: A phone call came a couple of weeks ago bringing a request from a gentleman who identified himself as "one of your fans." I guess that means there are at least two. "Why don't you reprint that Easter column you did several years ago, the one called 'True Confessions of a Great Lover.' I sort of liked that."

My immediate reaction was, "Hey, why haven't I thought of that before? Maybe we could do that every week or so; it would certainly lighten the load."

I looked back and found that I still believe what that column said, so here it is, with a new twist or two added for good measure. The original appeared in the Arkansas Gazette, *April 21, 1984.)*

We humans just won't leave Easter alone. We try to explain it, but we can't. We make words and fiddle with them, but they won't come out right. We try to do the day justice, but we fail. We should know better, but obviously we don't. Or perhaps it's that we simply can't give up trying to capture the glory.

But Easter is not an event to be captured and explained. It's an experience to be celebrated. It's a gift to be received, a jewel to be admired. Easter is a grand proclamation to be affirmed, a burst of glory set amidst the beauty of spring. Easter is the Creator's word that humanity's final enemy has been overcome. Easter is the ultimate message of hope.

Easter!

Who could remain silent in the presence of such an event! Even the stones cry out. Every flowering bush shouts for joy.

Perhaps our problem with Easter is that we've failed to see the grand event as the true confession of a great lover. The day is exactly that: Easter is the truest, fullest confession of the greatest of all lovers. Easter is the grand proclamation of the Creator's total affection for all creation.

For Christians, the resurrection is the dramatic reaffirmation of God's unending love affair with all that has been created. As with all lovers, God long ago learned that mere prose, the unadorned word, is never adequate to convey love's message. Proclamation and prophecy are fine, but we suspect that most humans have found that poetry is better and that music is better still.

And another point: God knows that when it comes to expressing love, nothing can surpass presence; nothing can match incarnation. Easter is the Creator's ultimate confirmation that nothing, not even death, can terminate the kind of love expressed in the Incarnation.

Easter's specialty is to overcome death—in whatever form death may occur. Easter speaks a saving word, a "resurrection" word, to death—whether it's the death of faith or hope or love or relationships or trust in other human beings. Or whether it's the death that is militarism and racism and bigotry and injustice and other sins.

Easter greets all death with resurrection. It brings the grandest good news.

Easter is renewed hope and rekindled faith. Easter is sunrise. Easter is the perfect gift for those who have everything. Or nothing.

—*Arkansas Gazette*, April 14, 1990.

6

Advent Waiting

It's true. There's no time quite like Advent. Such a claim could be made for each religious season, I suspect, of whatever faith. Every religious observance has its own specialness. For Advent, that specialness has to do with waiting. Yet waiting isn't quite the right word. There is waiting—and there is *waiting*.

There is a waiting that is little more than despair, an expression of hopelessness. There is waiting that is tedious. There is waiting that generates impatience, that manufactures boredom, that leaves one exhausted.

And then there is Advent waiting. Advent infuses waiting with a new and deeper dimension, a divine dimension. Advent waiting is waiting charged with anticipation, sweetened with hope, blessed with conviction, affirmed in faith, and confirmed in experience.

Advent waiting is waiting marked by silent wonder and joy. Advent waiting ties us to our past. It unites us with our most essential, most fundamental roots. Advent waiting reminds us who we are. Advent waiting recalls an ancient pronouncement. It speaks of a promise. It foretells a grand, glorious gift.

Advent waiting brings good news from a far country, from an ancient time. Advent waiting warms the present and brightens the future with a light first struck in a distant past and not yet extinguished. Those who walk in darkness have seen a great light. Advent reminds us that hope springs eternal.

Advent waiting is both passive and active. It is passive in that it invites quiet contemplation, meditation, and anticipation. It is active in that it is "busy" waiting. It is energized waiting. It is a time of preparing, of getting ready.

Advent waiting is exhilarated waiting. It is waiting buoyed by confident expectation. It is waiting whose reward is both promised through faith and confirmed by reality.

Advent waiting yields multiple blessings. It nurtures the heart's better intentions. It restores lost hope. It heals wounded relationships. It soothes the most bitter hurts—loss, pain, fear, and despair. Advent waiting nurtures love.

Advent is the great restorer of faith. Advent bids us to trust God and, therefore, to have greater faith in our fellow humans. Furthermore, Advent's promise is so grand that it encompasses the whole of creation. It speaks of harmony and peace within the entire order of things.

Advent speaks of a gift so grand that it must be celebrated with the best we have. That includes our rituals, our songs and music, our silences, our symbols, our poetry, and our prose. Advent merits the best waiting we can offer.

—*Arkansas Gazette,* December 8, 1990.

7

The Perils and Joys of Spring

It's that time of the year again. That time when a few scattered worshipers are apt to march into church just as the preacher is standing up to pronounce the benediction.

Tomorrow being the first day of daylight saving time, we are well advised to heed the familiar annual reminder: Before you go to bed tonight, set your clocks forward one hour. (I think that's right, but you'd better check me out on this. I got it wrong one year and showed up for church an hour early. But I guess I needed it.)

Anyway, something regarding time happens early tomorrow morning and it's bound to confuse a bunch of people, one way or another. To say nothing of how it's likely to mess up the rest of creation.

Old-timers will remember that when this whole daylight-saving business began, some farmers were hopping mad about it. They said their hens wouldn't know when to lay or their cows when to give milk. Those farmers argued that it was dumb and probably downright blasphemous to mess this way with Mother Nature.

But whatever, daylight saving time is here once again and I, for one, am glad. I love it. How great it is to have those longer evenings! How grand that after supper there's still time to go outdoors while it's still daylight, putter around in the yard awhile, maybe take a walk, watch the evening come, and revel in the beauty of another day as you do your best to grow old gracefully.

The long-awaited arrival of daylight saving time is surely one of the grand events of the season. It's a confirmation that spring is, in fact, here. With the days suddenly an hour longer, life takes on a wondrous new dimension, an added excitement.

Lives there a people with souls so dead who never to themselves have said, "This is my own, my native daylight saving time"? If there be such a people, God pity them.

Ah, the coming of spring.

Ah, dogwoods. Ah, redbuds. Ah, azaleas. And forsythias and japonicas and wisterias. Ah, all blooming things. Would that all life could be as pleasant as those delightful hours of longer spring days. Days that whisper their hints that lazy summer evenings, with their own mystical magic, can't be far away.

One day of spring is enough to convince the most skeptical: God—if nobody else around this place—is still doing things right.

Perhaps this is one of the great lessons of spring: We humans would do well to observe, study, and ponder the ways of the Creator. A popular wisdom advises us to "do what we do best." What God does best is testified to each spring morning.

In spring, the land (and all creation, it seems) is renewed. Restored. Healed. Made right. When was the last time we humans did anything half so grand as what we observe during a single day in spring?

Spring is our classroom. The Creator is our teacher. Homework has been assigned and there'll be a test. And just think: Come tomorrow, there'll be an extra hour of lovely daylight during which we may do our work. (And our play.)

—*Arkansas Gazette,* April 6, 1991.

CHAPTER IV

Getting Read to Ramble

He who would travel happily must travel light.
—Antoine de Saint-Exupery (1939)

1

Young Enough to Gallivant

It was a small question, a simple question, an innocent question. Asked during one of our evening walks, my wife and I. Through the park; around by Stoby's; back home. A daily ritual.

A lovely evening. Nice cool breeze. Hello to neighbors.

A small question. Simple. Innocent. "Do you think I really look sixty-five years old?" That was me. A few days after my birthday. That birthday upon which, as I'd been rather abruptly reminded, I'd become "a ward of the state." A new Medicare cardholder.

We'd just walked through bunches of happy people playing in the park. Children running fifty miles an hour; handsome young men and beautiful young women jogging; athletic people, young and old alike, playing softball, tennis, soccer. Sweating people.

"Do you think I really look sixty-five?" Did I already ask that or did I just imagine I did? Oh, well.

I don't think it was my wife's answer that set me back so much as the speed with which she delivered. It came lightning fast, almost before I'd affixed the question mark: "Yes."

"Yes what?"

"Yes to your question. Yes, I think you look sixty-five."

"Oh."

Another half block.

Another block.

"No kidding now, seriously—do you really, honestly think I look sixty-five years old?" That was me again, grasping for a straw.

Long pause. Still walking. Birds stop singing.

"You're not going to cry, are you?" That was Liz, getting me ready.

She continued, this time more thoughtfully, as though she, too, had noticed all those vigorous young people doing all those exhausting exercises: "Well, considering all you've been through . . ."

I interrupted: "You mean like this marriage?"

"No, I mean all that sickness. All that."

"Oh. Yeah. I forgot about all that. Well, maybe so."

And besides, I thought to myself, what's so bad about looking sixty-five years old? At least I had sense enough to marry an honest woman.

I told Liz the conversation reminded me of our Methodist bishop friend who once told a congregation how much he and his wife enjoyed their evening walks. A relaxing time, the bishop said. A quiet time. A peaceful time.

"She goes on Tuesdays and I go on Thursdays," the bishop had said. (Yes, I've told you that one before, but I'm getting old.)

But whatever, the subject has larger dimensions. Why all this concern about how old we look? Why so much ado about so little a thing as how many lines one might have on one's face, or how many hairs one may not have on one's head, or whatever other signs of age?

It's all been said before, but it bears repeating: Age isn't a matter of years so much as it is of attitude. And besides, what's so bad about age, anyway? The last of life for which the first was made. John Denver sings about it: It turns him on to think of growing old. Me, too.

I know people scarce out of their teens who are old. I also know bunches of people who carry Medicare cards—like the one I've just recently placed, so grudgingly, in my own wallet—who are young. (I feel like an impostor, carrying that card. Who, me? On Medicare?)

Anyway, I'm old enough to say this with conviction and joy: When I die, if I ever do, I just hope I die young. And so far, it's looking good. Right now I'm going to quit this silly work and go outside and play.

—*Arkansas Democrat-Gazette*, July 18, 1992.

First Aid Kit

I heard it on the radio. Some fellow talking about what a tough time businesses, both small and large, are having "during this time of pain and change."

An appropriate topic indeed. Appropriate not only for businesses, but for ordinary folks as well. How are any of us, individuals and groups alike, to make it through "times of pain and change"?

The phrase made me think. It's true that for many, the present is indeed a time of pain and change. But when has it ever been otherwise? We can count on it: It's always the case that for some folks, somewhere in this world, the moment at hand is a time of pain and change.

But, anyway, this is one of the risks of listening to the radio—unless you stick with rap music, you're apt to have to think.

In the instance noted above, the comment prompted a mental game. I tried to recall those phrases we humans have used, at one time or another, to characterize our times. The following came to mind: *The best of times; the worst of times. The days of wine and roses. The winter of our discontent. The springtime of life. The dark night of the soul. The good old days. The times that try men's souls. Our salad days.*

And so on. It seems we're always living in some kind of "times." Good times. Bad times. Tough times. Happy times. Hard times. Carefree times. Huckleberry Finn's friend Jim got it right when he told Huck's fortune: "Considerable troubles; considerable joys."

All of which leads to the question of the day: Is there some philosophy of life—some type of outlook, some rule for living—that can equip a person for whatever type of "times" life might offer?

It's an always-timely question. Here's an attempted response. Herewith some things to include in one's kit bag as one ventures forth on this journey called life:

A generous supply of faith. The word *faith* means different things to different people, and that's okay. Faith in God; faith in the workings of the universe; faith in one's fellow persons. I'll not dictate what faith should mean for you. Write your own definition. But about this be sure: Faith is essential for the journey. Don't leave home without it.

A healthy portion of awe. Take along an inexhaustible supply of wonder and excitement—a passion to celebrate life's mystery, miracle, and majesty. Don't assume you're required to understand it all. Be equipped to stand amazed in the presence of life.

A pinch of doubt. Don't be afraid of your doubts. Make friends with doubt. Be willing to question life. Doubt, as it leads to inquiry, is often the best door to growth. A closed mind, like a closed heart, is no compliment—and certainly no joy—to the Creator.

A couple of bushels of humor. Pity the poor traveler condemned to journey with those who have no sense of humor! Laugh with others—and at yourself. Why I feel most sorry for God: Having to put up with all those religious folks who have absolutely no sense of humor. Poor God.

A full helping of respect for—and not just tolerance of—the religious views of others. Travel as one who lives as a servant, not as a master.

—*Arkansas Democrat-Gazette,* September 12, 1992.

3

Plan Ahead—Then Plan Ahead Again

Well, it's mid-July again and you know what that means. It means it's time for our annual "What We Did on Our Vacation" report.

(I don't enjoy this any more than you do, but it's something I've got to go through with, a habit I can't break. It's sort of like sinning, I suppose, though I really don't know much about that, either. Anyway, I'll try to drop something religious into this to justify your effort.)

"What I Did on My Vacation" by John S. Workman. Grade: Retired.

First off, I suppose I ought to explain that retired people do indeed take vacations. In fact, retired people probably need vacations more than normal people do. And besides, somebody's got to wear all those Hawaiian shirts, bright green trousers, big sun hats, and trendy tennis shoes. It's not fair to expect ordinary humans to do those things all by themselves.

Second off, one just doesn't up and take a summer vacation. There's a lot of ritual involved, most notably prevacation planning. For me, this year's ritual centered on two major elements: One—deciding, after prolonged agonizing, to not buy a newer car for our trip to the Northeast to visit family. I opted, rather, for a brand-new set of tires for my old and faithful friend, the Silver Adventurer, our '86 Ford Escort station wagon.

(You need to know all this, so keep reading.)

I cinched my decision by also purchasing brand-new windshield wiper blades. I then took the bold step of replacing my standard car radio with the kind that plays cassette tapes. All of this means that I am now committed to keeping the Silver Adventurer for at least the next several decades.

(The cassette player, purchased primarily to listen to our son the opera singer, was a smart move, one I should have made five years ago, when I first began to ponder the idea. The player paid for itself, in enjoyment, within the first hundred miles of our journey. It also plays tapes by lesser singers, sermons, funny stories by Garrison Keillor, and recordings made on family trips of years ago. Great fun.)

The second prevacation ritual was deciding to build a wooden box to hold all those tools I always take on auto trips of ten miles or more from home. Old-timers will understand this compulsion. The box is a dandy, sturdy as a bank vault. Only there's a problem: It is so heavy our little car can barely move when it's aboard. I had to abandon the entire project. (I've since tried to give the box away but have had no takers.)

I see I'm almost out of space and haven't even gotten to our trip. Quickly a few highlights:

• A grand visit in New Jersey with our oldest son and his

family, which includes two of our four grandchildren. We've got photos.

• Attending, at Wolf Trap Farm Park for the Performing Arts, near Washington, an opera in which our youngest son sang the tenor lead. With us were our oldest son; my younger brother and wife, who came from Houston, Texas, for the event; and family friends, former Arkansans now living in Washington. A grand time.

• A homeward swing through South Carolina for an enjoyable visit with a brother-in-law and his family.

Now some justification for this rather selfish report. Time and again throughout our trip I thought of how, almost five years ago, I believed I'd never again have the joys that such occasions provide. A long and tough battle with cancer prompted such fears. You probably already know this, but think on it: Life is sweet. Enjoy it. Celebrate it each day. Even when it's not vacation time.

—*Arkansas Gazette,* July 20, 1991.

4

A Place to Be Brave

Actress Mary Steenburgen said it recently at Hendrix College in Conway, where she was awarded an honorary degree. With a refreshing candor, the Arkansas-born actress recalled that during her student days at Hendrix she avoided social gatherings, and that her performances in college dramas "were not particularly outstanding."

"But the stage gave me a place to be brave," Steenburgen said. What a significant observation. And what a marvelous discovery: A place to be brave!

Since hearing the comment a couple of weeks ago, its magic has lingered. A place to be brave. How grand to find one's place to be brave.

If life is indeed a stage and we all are players thereon, it follows—according to Steenburgen's experience—that just such a discovery can await each of us.

Life does, in fact, offer all of us some very special places to be brave. It may be in confronting the battles of ordinary everyday experiences; in contending against the pressures to conform, to compromise, to surrender. It may be in dealing with an illness. Or in trying to salvage a troubled relationship. It may be in fighting our own skirmishes in the drug war. Or it may be in doing battle in that other ever-continuing conflict—the one in which ethics and morality are constantly in peril.

You name it: Whatever societal problem could be mentioned, it follows that life offers us places to be brave.

What does it mean to be brave in our time? Unfortunately, bravery is a quality associated more with the battlefield than with ordinary everyday life. But in the absence of a shooting war to inspire pursuit of the red badge of courage, where is bravery to find its playing field?

Where else if not in the home. And the workplace. And in government. In the legislature.

A special kind of bravery is needed for our time. It is a bravery that has less to do with the adrenaline glands and more to do with the brain. And the heart. Needed is the kind of bravery that gives legislators the wisdom, as well as the guts, to put public interest above special interest; to know how to measure values; to know what is right and what is wrong; to know what is of lasting worth and what is of passing interest. Needed is the kind of bravery that makes statesmen out of politicians.

From whence comes such bravery? Among its sources is belief. And conviction. And faith. And love. Once again a discovery: The human spirit is nourished by religious faith.

Life is a tough, exciting voyage. Other than the brave may apply, but the brave will best weather and most enjoy the trip. And only the brave can make the ride worth writing home about.

—*Arkansas Gazette,* November 4, 1989.

5

Picky, Picky, Picky

It was never intended, in the divine scheme of things, that a perfectionist should be called upon to rake leaves.

Think about it: You rake one spot of your yard perfectly clean, carefully and painstakingly removing each and every solitary leaf and placing it, ever so neatly, in a perfect little pile with its fellows. And then you move on to the next spot and do the same perfect job again.

But then, quite suddenly, along comes a gust of wind straight out of Hades and messes up your whole playhouse! A leaf explosion! You can hardly recognize those areas you'd left so neat, so leaf-free. The whole bloomin' task has to be done all over again. And probably again. It's just not right. If there were really a God in heaven, the wind wouldn't blow when you rake leaves. It'd wait. But it doesn't.

Yes, I know—it's the leaf raker, not the wind, who's supposed to do the waiting. But by the time I work up the mood to rake leaves, I've got to move fast, wind or no wind. The mood doesn't linger.

But we were talking about perfectionists.

Let's face it: Life has always been hard on us perfectionists, tough breed though we be. We want things done right, and we want to do things right. And the world, most of it, anyway, seems it couldn't care less whether or not things are done right—whether we're talking about leaf raking, brain surgery, or soul saving.

Or, for that matter, running a country. Which brings us to president-elect Bill Clinton. Oh, yes—in case you haven't heard, our governor, on last Tuesday, was elected president of the United States. You need to know that. And what an event! What a happening! Our governor comes on as a man who wants to do it right. That's not only good, that's great.

Three cheers for Bill! Three cheers for Hillary! Five cheers for Chelsea! God bless each of them. God give them strength for the task.

But what has all this to do with us perfectionists? A lot. And since everyone who reads this page is an especially holy person—totally committed to being perfect in all things—here are a couple of areas ripe for attention at this significant moment in history, this beginning of a new national administration:

Lifestyles. In a country where overconsumption, material affluence, and greed have been the dominant forces—leaving many on the fringes, outcast, homeless, and hungry—it seems there should be a community of people devoted to living "truly religious" lifestyles.

But isn't that mixing religion and politics? No, it isn't. It means, among numerous other things, making conscious and deliberate choices to live in accordance with the highest moral and ethical ideals of one's faith, one's core beliefs.

It means that in this affluent nation, religiously sensitive people will put renewed emphasis on living as good stewards. Living as good neighbors. Living simply. Living frugally. Conserving resources. It means being aware of living in a global village where all people have responsibilities toward each other. It means making a sincere effort to "live simply in order that others may simply live."

Values. In addition to its "witnessing" role, the religious community has a "remembering" role. It is called to be the community's "rememberer." To call us all to remember that it is in our religious traditions and values that we best discover who we are, whose we are, and what it is we are called to be and to do.

The times call for efforts to do it right. Even efforts to do it perfect. The time calls for moral and ethical perfectionists.

Picky, picky, picky.

Oops—there goes the wind again, messing up my leaf piles! I'm outta here.

—*Arkansas Democrat-Gazette,* November 7, 1992.

6

Lifestyles of the Nutty Rich

I don't know exactly how to do this, but it's got to be done, so let's get at it. What I've got to say here is difficult to put into print, but it's the right thing to do, so here goes.

I actually had a good pecan crop this year.

It's the truth. Indeed, I had a dandy pecan crop this year. My five trees outdid themselves; or at least four of them did. I hate to reveal this, but my harvest filled five of those giant-sized heavy-duty paper shopping bags. And there are still more nuts to gather.

The end result is that I am now a pecan-affluent person. I am pecan rich. Pecan filthy rich. And therein lies the problem. Or a whole bunch of problems.

Problem No. 1: I'm not exactly accustomed to being rich. I'm not sure I know how to do it. How to handle it. Bigger barns have come to mind. Or at least a bigger freezer. And perhaps fudge, with double nuts, twice every week. Brownies every other evening. Pecan pies after breakfast, lunch, and supper. Every day.

Let the good times roll. Pecan roll.

Problem No. 2: If all my kinfolks, neighbors, and friends learn of my pecan wealth, you know what that'll mean. They'll expect me to actually give them whole bunches of my pecans. Buckets full of my very own pecans.

Just think about this problem I've got. If these people find out how I've been blest, I'll have to give away bags and bags of my precious pecans; my pecans that taste so heavenly with chocolate; my pecans I've watched grow through three seasons, anticipating their abundant harvest. All just for me.

All of which brings us to Problem No. 3, expressed here in some theological questions:

Why does God do this to me? Why does my good fortune have to occur during the very season when my preacher and Sunday school teacher, and almost everyone else, are telling me how much more blessed it is to give than to receive? Why couldn't I have become rich in, say, July, when almost nobody thinks, much less talks aloud, about the constraints of religion?

Now I've got to consider actually giving away whole bunches of my luscious pecans. Most of them cracked—and some even picked out—by hand. By my hands, I might add. (Did you ever sit for hours picking out zillions of munchy pecans all the while knowing that you were actually going to give away all those goodies? It's too much.)

So there you have it. Don't tell me that us rich folks don't have our problems.

Okay, now the sermon. Possibly you've already picked up on this: What we've got here is a real problem. A genuine problem, one as old as humanity. The problem of self. Self-centeredness. Selfishness. Greed. Avarice. Cupidity. Voracity. Rapacity. Covetousness. Ravenousness. Possessiveness. Number Oneness.

They're all here, in one form or another, in our pecan problems. And for a while there I thought this was just about pecans. I thought all those pecans were supposed to be just for me. All mine. To keep. To have all to myself.

But along came Advent. And something called the Christmas spirit. And there went my pecans.

—*Arkansas Democrat-Gazette,* December 7, 1991.

7

An Offer You Can't Refuse

It was, as best as I recall, about three months—perhaps four—but it seemed like a year. The time that elapsed between that day, many decades ago, I ordered the first new car I ever purchased and the day that it was delivered.

An eternity of waiting. An eternity of floor-pacing and fit-sleeping. An eternity of reviewing the brochures, looking at the pictures. An eternity of wondering if I'd be caught if I sneaked down to the car dealer's, hid around the corner, and watched for that big truck to roll in, that truck that would be carrying my new car!

Ah, yes, anticipation. Ah, yes, the agony of anticipation.

I haven't purchased bunches of new cars in my lifetime, but on those few occasions I have, it's been a major event. Something on the order of deciding whether or not to fund the B-1 bomber. For someone who takes a minimum of six weeks to muster up enough courage to invest in a new pair of shoes, buying a new car is an experience not unlike Columbus's decision to sail off the edge of the world. Only for Columbus, the decision was easier.

Such thoughts came this week as, at least 30,000 miles ahead of my carefully planned schedule, I in fact traded cars. Got me a new one, I did. Got us a new one, that is.

Well, not exactly a new one, but a practically new one. A '92 model, just a few months old and already broken in. With only 9,097 miles! (I'm sort of like royalty, those folks who hire food tasters. My last two "new" cars have been tested by other people.)

But anyway, there's still enough new-car smell in my previously rented vehicle—and not a scratch or a smudge to reveal my secret—to convince even my mother-in-law that John has, in fact, actually bought her daughter a brand new car! Some son-in-law, that John.

But let me squirm a bit. Our old car, which we'd had for six years, was signaling that it wanted to retire. So, one morning last week I actually picked up the phone and informed my friendly Ford dealer of my zany plan. Could he find me a new Taurus wagon, preferably "that coffee-and-milk color."

"That's mocha brown," my car-dealer friend said. And yes, he thought he could. He'd call me. Another yes. He'd found my car, but it had a few more extras than I'd planned. More extras than I'm worthy of, actually. And the price was only umpteen jillion dollars or two of my grandchildren.

Would I want to look at a '92 model the agency had used as a rental car? It wasn't mocha brown—it was white—but it could be acquired at quite a nice savings. Indeed I would want to look at it.

All of which is to tell you that, unlike the three months I had to wait for my first new automobile, the waiting time for this one was considerably less. I looked at the car at 9:30 that morning, had to go from Conway to Little Rock for a meeting at noon, got back at midafternoon, and before closing time the deal was done! Lapsed waiting time: About six hours. But hear this—those six hours weren't a whole lot shorter than the three months I waited for my first new car.

But hold on here. This is supposed to be a religion column. Where's the religion in all this?

I really don't know. But I do know this: There's something so marvelously exciting about buying a new car that there's bound to be some sort of religious dimensions to the whole experience.

Think about it: There's anticipation, excitement, wonder, delight, and joy. I don't know about you, but it seems to me that if we don't feel all those emotions about our religion, we ought to.

—*Arkansas Democrat-Gazette*, October 10, 1992.

CHAPTER V

Rules of the Road

If an ass goes traveling, he'll not come home a horse.
—Thomas Fuller, M.D. (1732)

1

Things It's Okay to Forget

I thought I was doing pretty good just to remember to give the clerk the discount coupon. The supermarket clerk. The one in the Cash Only No Checks express lane. The clerk who had just spent twenty minutes, or so it seemed, helping the lady in front of me write a check. The lady who couldn't find her driver's license. During which time I kept trying to convince myself how much God actually loved these people anyway—a point of theology which, at the moment, I found rather difficult to abide.

But to resume this little tale. Throughout my one-mile hike to the supermarket I'd rehearsed the three things I needed to remember: Buy the toothpaste; buy the chocolate candy; give the checkout lady the coupon for the toothpaste.

So far so good. I'd remembered it all. Liz would be so proud of me.

But how was I supposed to know that I was going to have to make change? And correct change at that. Don't these people know I'm retired? Don't they know that it was just such things as this—remembering grocery lists, getting stuck in express checkout lanes, having to make change—that hastened my retirement?

"That'll be $4.27, sir," the nice young lady said, smiling. No problem, I thought to myself. I was totally calm. Composed. Only there was a problem. I guess that all my life I've known that a quarter is twenty-five cents. Only this time, when I counted my money aloud, the quarter came out as twenty cents. Every time I counted, that quarter came out as twenty cents. And no matter how carefully and repeatedly the young lady explained it to me, that quarter registered, in my head, as twenty cents. You explain it—I can't.

Anyway, the young lady, who probably attended one of the church-related colleges in our town (she was so especially nice and patient), finally helped me see the light, much to the relief of the restless masses in line behind me, who by this time had just about expended their daily minimum requirement of good behavior.

On my hike back home, which by now had grown to about five miles, the experience got me to sort of thinking. And that was another thing I'd wanted to get away from in retirement. Thinking. But it was no use. I thought anyway. Even though I am retired.

"Workman, how in the world are you religious people going to save this planet when you can't even make correct change in the supermarket? How in the world are you going to function in a confusing and complex society, a society filled with sharp folks—folks, a lot of them, anyway, who actually know how to make correct change? How are you religious people going to make it in the grown-up world?

Tough questions, those. Especially during a fifteen-mile hike home after being humiliated in the supermarket.

But there were other thoughts, too. Thoughts about things that it just might be okay to forget—and things that one should never, ever forget. Here are some of the latter, some things that religious people must never ever forget:

How to love. A popular song says it: "Some say love, it is a razor that leaves the heart to bleed. . . . I say love, it is a flower, and you its only seed." This never forget: How to bloom where you're planted.

How to keep faith. The world can forget lots of things so long as it remembers how to keep faith. Perhaps the most valuable gift the biblical religions offer is their role as humanity's "rememberers." Authentic religion helps the world remember how to keep faith.

How to do good deeds. Never belittle a good deed done in love. Never underestimate the power of a word spoken in kindness, a relationship mended, a bond strengthened.

However, it'd still be sort of nice to be able to make correct change in the supermarket. Especially with the whole world watching.

—*Arkansas Democrat-Gazette*, May 2, 1992.

2

On Getting the Soup "Just Right"

It's another of those many things I've always wondered about: On the side of the soup can, where it says to stir the water into the soup "slowly," just what does that mean? Slowly according to whom? Southern slowly? Northern slowly? Or does it mean really s-l-o-o-o-w-l-y. It's confusing. And if I'm going to get the soup right I need to know what they mean.

I'm not too handy in the kitchen—a sandwich and a simple dish or two and perhaps an omelet—so I need to know how to get the soup right. It's important to me, getting the soup right. For theological reasons. When, as they say, my time comes, I don't want to be turned away at the Pearly Gates because I stirred the soup too quickly.

"Sorry," Mr. Workman, you didn't get the soup right. Too fast. Tough break."

But anyway, soup-can directions pose an interesting line of thought—at least they do if you're retired or otherwise just naturally lazy. That line of thought: There are some things in this life that need to be done slowly. And there are other things that need to be done quickly.

"Be quick to give your hand but slow to give your heart," goes an old saying. I suppose that's still pretty sound advice. Here are a few other things that could bear being done quickly:

Getting rid of a grudge
Mopping up the paint after you've spilled it on the carpet
Offering—and accepting—forgiveness
All known forms of medical examinations

On the other hand, some things need to be done slowly, such as:

Making fudge
Building lasting relationships
Raising children successfully
Raising parents successfully—or at least just raising them, period

Life, dear friends, is like making soup. Sometimes the directions don't tell us all we need to know. Sometimes we get it right; sometimes we don't. Sometimes we alone must bear all the blame. But sometimes the fault is not entirely our own—we can blame people who use unclear words like *slowly* in the directions.

But always, even if we mess up the soup, we have to go ahead on anyway, as another saying goes. It's during our soup-spoiling times, I submit, that we come about as close as we possibly can to discovering one of life's most valuable, if most difficult, lessons: If we're going to get it right, we've got to keep trying. Stay at it. Try it again. Keep stirring. Maybe slower this time. Maybe faster.

There's another thing about this business of making soup: There are other people who yearn for us to get it right. It's important to these people simply because it's important to us. What they feel for us is something called love. They want us to get the soup right for a simple, yet profound reason: They love us.

So—let's keep stirring. Sooner or later we're bound to get close. And who knows. One day we might even get it right.

—*Arkansas Gazette,* September 14, 1991.

3

Biggest Winner Has Doubts

Since in a few short weeks I could be so unbearably rich I wouldn't be speaking to you ordinary poor people, perhaps I'd better get some things said. You see, I've been personally selected by American Family Publishers as "the brand-new $20 million winner [who has] just been found in Arkansas!"

I learned this and a lot more from a personal letter I recently received from Ed McMahon, the television personality and super-giveaway person. Surely Ed is the most generous gent in history, the man whose blessings are sought more eagerly than those of Pope John Paul II, Billy Graham, and the Dalai Lama combined.

The announcement is in giant print: "John Workman of Arkansas—the biggest winner in history—will be awarded the full $20 million prize on national television by NBC's Ed McMahon!"

Is this a great country or what?

The only thing I have to do is return the prizewinning number by January 22. But I can tell by that sly smile on Ed's face—he sent me his picture—that he already knows: I'm the winner.

There are problems, however. I'm on Social Security and not allowed to assemble more than twenty-five dollars, I think it is (or something like that), in a single year. My new $20 million would probably be noticed.

Anyway, I've decided not to accept Ed's truly generous offer. It's not that I couldn't use the cash. If I applied it to my annual medical insurance premiums, I might be able, given time, to come up with the balance. Or I could use the money to make some of my long-patient creditors happy.

Okay, let's get serious.

No, I'll not play this game, even though it could cost me something called $20 million, whatever that is. Sure—if I'm too noble to keep the filthy lucre for myself I could give it to charity.

What in the world could be worth more than a shot at $20 million? I suggest there are such things, and they include the chance to do the following:

> To make even a small protest against a society that teaches its children that "things" are more to be desired than values—moral, spiritual, human values.
>
> To interject an old but never popular idea: It is possible to gain the world and lose the soul.
>
> To refuse to be part of the "lottery theory" of life—that one's deliverance depends on chance and good fortune rather than on will, work, effort for the common good, and faith in God.
>
> To refuse to excuse society from its just obligations; to refuse to substitute "chance" for justice. Just as charity can be used to "go bail for justice"—that as long as we are charitable we don't have to be "just"—so the sweepstakes, lottery, and prize mentality keep society from fulfilling its just responsibilities to its own.

That in a day when millions of East Europeans are looking for new values, we in the West might send a message that democracy and freedom are more than a chance at some easy money.

Silly me—to think that such ideals are worth more than $20 million.

—*Arkansas Gazette*, January 6, 1990.

4

Patio Picnic Prompts Practical Preaching

It was table talk. The type of conversation husbands and wives have at mealtime. While enjoying our usual noonday picnic on the patio, the conversation turned, mid-sandwich, to projects yet to be done around the house. A frequent topic, it seems.

Among the priorities: Perhaps now that the leaf-raking season is at hand, it'd be nice if someone (guess who) could get around to fixing a proper arrangement for our compost heap. Not a particularly appropriate mealtime topic, I'll admit.

"That shouldn't be too big a project, should it?" That was Liz, asking.

A few more bites on my sandwich. Pondering.

Some chips. A slice of apple. Several swallows of iced tea.

"Well, in order for me to do this right, I'll have to buy some treated wood, dig the holes for those post things—the posts that will support the heavy wire mesh that I'll have to buy—and then I'll have to buy some more wire to make the siding; and then. . . ."

"Oh, does it take all that?" That was Liz, interrupting, munching a Democratic potato chip (no *e*).

"Well, if I'm going to do it right it does indeed take all that," I responded, rather heatedly, my traditional chocolate dessert cookie in mouth.

"But does it really have to be done right?"

That was Liz, with the response I'd expected and for which I was ready. (After all, she certainly couldn't have forgotten—though she was considerate enough not to mention it—that I'd sort of promised, every year for the past five years, to get this project done.)

"Does it have to be done right?" I shot back. "You're asking me if this project has to be done right? Why, certainly this project has to be done right!"

That was me responding indignantly, as though I were a graduate expert, cum laude, on the morality of compost heap construction. "You bet your Fig Newton Lite dessert cookie this project has to be done right!"

It was at this point that I proceeded to practice some serious patio preaching, though not before begging for, and being granted, a second chocolate cookie. "That's the trouble with this whole world, honey—too many people who think that things don't have to be done right! Good heavens! Yes, this compost thing has to be done right!" So there.

With that I concluded my sermon, though not before having worked up an appetite for yet one more chocolate dessert cookie. Preaching is hard work.

Now some post-sermon commentary. There are, of course, some things that ought to be done righter—or more right—than others. Compost heaps are important, but I'll admit they're not real high on the list of things that really need to be done right.

The thought is prompted: What, then, are those things in this weary old world that need to be done really, really right? There certainly must be a long list of such things, but it seems the following should be included:

Parenting. It's not the only factor, of course, but I suspect that inadequate parenting is one of the major elements in the many social problems evidenced among young people these days. Parenting deserves to be done right.

Neighboring. Meaning what? Meaning how to be a better citizen, both in the neighborhood at hand and in the larger world community. Being a good neighbor—socially, politically, ecologically—is an important and difficult task, one that deserves being done right.

Governing. And, more to the seasonal point, politicking. Both need to be done right. Clean up America? You bet. And do it right.

—*Arkansas Democrat-Gazette,* September 26, 1992.

5

The Gods See Everywhere

When it first hit me it seemed like a good idea. Paint the closet in the guest bedroom. That was before I got hit the second time—by the realization of what it was I had gotten myself into. A mess is what it was. A two-week mess.

I'll save some words here. Being in a room for guests, of which we don't have many, this closet is a logical place to store stuff. You know, stuff not good enough to use but too good to throw away. Perhaps you know the problem.

Anyway, I wasn't long into my project before I got hit a third time: In order to paint a closet, it first becomes necessary to remove the contents. I probably should have realized that. If this sounds easy—removing the contents—I suggest you take a look at your own guest room closet.

Anyway again, that's what I did. Removed the contents. All of them. And that was probably the toughest part of the whole undertaking. No, on second thought that wasn't the toughest part. But I'm getting ahead of myself.

Behold, I show you a mystery: How the contents of one small closet can, when unpacked, overflow an entire room at least nine times the size of the closet! It's amazing. It probably has something to do with air hitting long-stored objects.

Anyway yet again, it was at about this point that I got hit a fourth time, which seems a bit much to require of a retired senior citizen. "Before you paint the closet, John, you've got to fill in all those nail holes, dents, scrapes, and scratches. Remember: The gods see everywhere."

Being a Methodist, I am naturally eager to do whatever is necessary to please the gods, so I filled every scratch. Finally to the easy part. Painting.

But not quite yet. "You know, John"—that voice again—"if you're really going to do this right, you need to build some more shelves. To properly store your treasures." Hit No. 5.

But we need to get on with this; we've got some moralizing to do. I'll have to trust your imagination to complete this little drama.

The moralizing: Getting these lives of ours in shape, and keeping them that way, is sort of like painting a closet. Before we can get to the easy part, there's a bunch of stuff that has to be done first. It's sort of a Murphy's Law of Human Interior Decorating.

Here are a couple of rules of the road regarding such a law:

Rule One: There are things we need to keep and things we need to toss.

Human interior decorating isn't just a matter of covering up the bumps and scratches. It involves some unpacking. Some unloading. Deciding what to keep and what to throw away is the tough part. Although friends and religious resources may help, the deciding is up to us.

Rule Two: Closet cleaning requires a maintenance contract.

It'd be nice if our closets would always stay clean and neatly painted. It'd be keen if our storerooms would forever stay straightened, if our desks would remain cleared, if our letter-answering would stay caught up, if our lives would always be neat and tidy. But it doesn't work that way. Perhaps we humans are sort of like New York City—we're forever under construction.

This business of living is like closet cleaning and painting in yet another fashion. After our work is done, we feel a whole lot better. So much better, in fact, that we can probably even make it until the next time, when it all has to be done yet once again.

Have a nice day.

—*Arkansas Democrat-Gazette*, February 8, 1992.

6

"Yeah, But Was He Talking About Pecans?"

What I've got to do, see, is get home quick after Sunday school and pick up all my pecans before the Episcopalians get out of church. Those Episcopalians right across the street from my house. That way it removes the temptation, to say nothing of it helping to keep my pecans right where God intended them to be.

One must remember that Episcopalians, not unlike Presbyterians and even an occasional Baptist, are only human. They aren't above gleaning a pecan or two from a neighbor's field— especially if that neighbor happens to be a Methodist who is in church two blocks away, totally immersed in Wesleyan morality. (Trust me on this. I know about this stuff.)

Of course, the Disciples of Christ are like this, too. As are even several Church of Christers and a few Pentecostals and maybe even a Catholic and an embarrassingly high percentage of some of those other brands you could mention.

Thank God for us mainline Methodists.

Okay—that's enough.

By now I trust you've got the message: There are still a couple of problems left for all of us do-gooders to solve. Among them is this business of greed and selfishness. (Yes, we've delivered this pecan sermon before, but judging from all the evidence, you must have been asleep. So fasten your pewbelts—here we go again.)

Ah, yes—greed and selfishness. Possessiveness, covetousness, hoggishness, voracity, avarice, and whatever other words express all those dreadful sins that afflict all you people out there. Thank God that history records no single instance in which a Methodist has been guilty of such low behavior.

(Whoops. Add to the list hypocrisy, self-righteousness, sanctimoniousness, haughtiness, Pharisaism, unctuousness—and, yes, just plain old lying.)

Now, with our common sins acknowledged, perhaps we can get

on with the discourse. What we've got here, dear friends, is a problem. I've got some pretty nice pecans on my five trees, and every instinct in my body urges me to hang on to them. I mean hang on to every last one of those pecans. If God had intended for all those other folks to have pecans, God would have put pecan trees in their yards, so there.

But wait a minute. Among the things they keep trying to teach me in Sunday school is that there is something wrong with this kind of thinking. I know that, of course. I know it with my head, but my heart (and my taste buds) still wrestle with "the pecan syndrome." Those organs want me to hang on to each one of those big, fat, juicy, delicious pecans, to have them all for myself. Woe is me. Who will deliver me from this terrible affliction?

Let's face it: Greed and selfishness are potent forces. Whether bold or subtle, they are capable of wielding terribly destructive forces within the human community.

Meanwhile, back in Sunday school, somebody has the gall to quote John Wesley on money: "Make all you can." (Amen to that, I say.) "Save all you can." (Preach on, Brother Wesley.) "Give all you can." (And that, as they say, is where he stopped preachin' and went to meddlin'.)

"Give all you can." Yeah—but was he talking about pecans?

—*Arkansas Gazette*, November 11, 1989.

7

The Joys of Being Lost

It was one of those brief items on the late-night TV news, a story about a new scientific development. The satellite-related device, currently used mostly in military applications but also suitable for civilian use, can give the precise location of any vehicle, vessel, or individual anywhere in the world. Think of it—one's precise location anywhere in the world!

The closing shot on the TV report showed the reporter, in a

construction hat with a small satellite dish mounted on top, saying, "You may never have to be lost again."

Think of that, John—you may never have to be lost again! If I'd heard that promise on the early-morning news, rather than late at night, I'd probably never have given it a second thought. But to tell a part-time theologian, just before he tries to drop off to sleep, that he may never have to be lost again—well, that can jolt you wider awake than a tree full of owls.

Never to be lost again. Just think of it.

There is, however, one small reservation regarding the gadget. It's accurate "only to within forty-eight feet." Well, that's not good enough. I know people who, if placed forty-eight feet squarely in front of their destination, would still be lost.

The reporter was, of course, speaking about geographical lostness, not theological lostness. (I absolutely will not, on this outing anyway, touch the theological dimensions of this subject. The implications are mind-boggling. Think of what it would do to this world's preachers if somebody discovered a device that would make it unnecessary for anyone, anywhere, ever to be "lost," in the biblical sense, again! Heaven forbid.)

But even speaking geographically, I'm not so sure it's good news that I may never have to be lost again. Truth to tell, I sort of enjoy the thought that I could be lost. To one who is the least bit adventurous and romantically inclined, it's a deeply disturbing thought that you need never be lost again; that no matter where you might roam across this whole wide Earth, or above it or underneath its seas, you need never again be lost.

To the romantic, that's not a pleasant thought. To know that one need never be lost again robs life of some of its most marvelous qualities—mystery, risk, adventure. Some of my favorite fantasies have to do with being lost. About how I, lost in the wilds and having to fight hordes of barbarians, save our little band of women and children. Always I'm the hero, saving the unprotected from the terrors of lostness.

I have in fact been lost, really lost geographically, only once in my life, and I can report that it is not a fun experience. Not during the occasion, anyway. My lostness occurred in the Rocky Mountains on a hiking trip. There were three of us—myself (a seasoned woodsman) and a couple of greenhorns who couldn't find their way forty-eight feet from home. We got lost. Really lost. And it was scary. But that's another story. Suffice it to say that some of the most important lessons I've learned in life I learned from that experience of being lost.

So, I'm going to try to forget that news report that it's now possible to never be lost again. I liked it better the old way—knowing that there was still some risk, still some mystery, still some lostness out there to be enjoyed.

—*Arkansas Gazette,* July 13, 1991.

CHAPTER VI

Passing Cypress Creek

*I should like to enjoy this summer
flower by flower,
as if it were to be the last one for me.*
—Andre Gide (1930)

Through the Valley of the Shadow

The following are two excerpts from the memory journal of a cancer patient. The first is dated April 1987, about two months after I underwent major surgery and just before I began a series of radiation and chemotherapy treatments that would extend throughout a full year.

If you can just make it from this bed to that bathroom door over there, John—that's seven steps!—you'll have reached your goal for the morning. Pull yourself together and do it. If you can.

This second excerpt is more recent, dated just this past October 3, 1991. It comes four years and eight months after the surgery mentioned above and three and a half years after completing eleven months of chemotherapy treatments; treatments that frequently left me too sick and too weak even to walk those seven steps across my bedroom.

Great going, John, you did it! A two-day bicycle camping trip from Conway to Petit Jean State Park and return. Seventy-five miles—you did it!

This story is about two things. First, it tells of one person's experience of recovering from major illness. Second, it is about fun. And adventure. Perhaps it is mostly about fun and adventure.

But these words are also an attempt to address a mystery: The uncertain and elusive role that adventure and fun might play in the complex and not yet fully understood process of healing.

Regarding medical matters, this writer is definitely a layperson. I do, however, have credentials: I am a recovering—and I would even dare to say recovered—cancer patient.

Like many cancer patients, I have of necessity learned more than a bit about my illness. That learning has come through conversations with doctors and other professionals in the medical and social

Author's note: Unlike the previous and following chapters, which are collections of basically unrelated essays, this chapter is of a whole. It is an expanded version of a feature article that originally appeared June 16, 1992, in the Arkansas Democrat-Gazette.

sciences. It has come through reading. And perhaps most significant of all, my learning about cancer has come through experience.

This I discovered early on: Cancer is "many diseases"—it can take many different forms—and no one person's case and experience is apt to be like another's. What is written here is based on my own experience and is not offered as applicable to every instance of cancer. But perhaps this one patient's experience may be helpful to others who face serious illness of whatever sort.

The First Week of January

It was during the first week of January 1987 that I was diagnosed as having leiomyosarcoma. I was told this was a rare and serious form of cancer that attacks the smooth muscle tissue surrounding an organ, rather than the organ itself.

Now it becomes necessary for you to learn more about me than you wanted to know. And more than I really want to tell you.

I was told I had a very large tumor—"approaching volleyball size," one doctor reported—in my lower pelvic region. Because of the tumor's size and the rarity of the type of cancer, I was advised to go to M. D. Anderson Hospital and Tumor Institute in Houston, the central component of the University of Texas System Cancer Center. There, in February 1987, I had surgery and was told, "No, your tumor wasn't volleyball size; it was basketball size."

When removing the tumor, it was found necessary also to remove my prostate gland and bladder. A portion of my intestines was used to construct a urinary diversion, routing the urine through a small hone, a "stoma," at my waistline, a few inches to the right of my naval.

I wear a plastic bladder, an external device that affords some distinction: I can explain to startled medical examiners and curious friends, "Yes, I donated my bladder to a bunch of needy Texans. And I threw in that prostate thing, too."

I was told that the urinary diversion device would "work just great" and would not impede my normal physical activities. I've found that to be true. Now at age sixty-four, I still engage in vigorous physical activities—do lots of yard work, chop and split firewood, walk a lot, ride my bicycle frequently, horse around with my grandchildren, and so on—and do most of the fun activities I enjoyed in my pre–plastic bladder years.

After the surgery in Texas I received my radiation and chemotherapy treatments in Arkansas. The thirty radiation treatments were given at Central Arkansas Radiation Therapy Institute, CARTI, in Little Rock. The chemotherapy treatments, which I received at home, were administered by my oncologist in Little Rock and by St. Vincent Infirmary Medical Center.

But enough medical talk. Let's get to the fun and adventure.

Let the Good Times Roll

October 2, 1991, 7:50 A.M.: You're on schedule, Workman—which means you're an hour late. Let's get this Great American Bicycle Venture on the road!

At last! Underway again with Old Jim, my faithful secondhand ten-speed bicycle, for which I paid twenty-five dollars some fifteen or so years ago. Old Jim, veteran of numerous pre-illness bike tours throughout Arkansas, also seems happy to be on the open road once again.

This long-planned and long-looked-forward-to trip is special to me. It's to celebrate two events in my life, both important to me: My sixty-fourth birthday (which actually was in July) and my recovery from cancer. *Laissez les bon temps rouler!* Let the good times roll!

For months after completing almost a year of chemotherapy, it was all I could do to go inside a hospital. The smells, sights, and sounds were too much. There were days following surgery and during my "chemo months" when I was deeply depressed. I despaired of faith, of hope, and almost of life itself. "Yea, though I walk through the valley of the shadow of death. . . ."

But many things kept me going. The love of family and friends, the resources of religious faith, the expert care and heartfelt concern of physicians and other health-care professionals, and my own commitment to following the prescribed treatments, though at times I hated them.

I also sought to invoke, and give full freedom to, those unknown and mysterious forces within that work for healing; forces which, I believe, are always on duty in the body and mind.

"Resilience." It is a word and a concept I thought of often. Of how the human body is such a marvelous, mysterious, wonderful creation. Of how it contains its own hospital; how it possesses its own inexplicable power to heal. The human body and mind—a marvelous piece of work indeed!

The Mountain and the Wind

Often in my mind, during the months before this bicycle trip, were thoughts of the mountain and the wind. Twice earlier I had pedaled Old Jim, heavy laden with camp gear, up the steep east end of Petit Jean Mountain. Twice I had sworn "Never again!" (But I didn't really mean it.)

This time, not yet one-third of the way up the mountain, I swore yet a third time: "Never, but never again, Workman, and you listen to me this time! Never again!" (I really didn't mean it this time, either.)

But we did it, Old Jim and I. I pedaled at least two-thirds of the way up, counting eight rest stops on the way. The other one-third of the way I pushed and pulled Jim, his thirty-five pounds of camp gear now feeling like a ton.

But at the top, the joy of victory—and the agony of the seat.

But we did it!

How long did it take, the trip from Conway to Petit Jean State Park? Seven and one-half hours. (The return trip, the following day, took five and one-half hours.)

Several months before this venture, and in anticipation of it—with visions of Petit Jean's steep east end in my head—I asked my chief bicycle mechanic and opera critic extraordinaire, seventy-eight-year-old Paul Matthews of Conway, if he could put a third sprocket wheel on my bike's crank. After cogitating a bit, Paul said it looked close, but he thought he could do it. And that it might even work.

He did and it did. The addition converted Old Jim from a ten-speed to a fifteen-speed. "Will this get me up Petit Jean Mountain?" I asked Paul in his outdoor shop, radio opera music in the background. "Man, with this thing you can pull stumps," was Paul's enthusiastic report.

Great, I thought to myself, I've got some stumps to pull.

There's a maxim in bicycle touring: No matter which way you're headed, the wind is always against you. Most of the time that's true. But not always. It's sort of like life: Sometimes it blesses, sometimes it bruises. But always it's there.

There are times, and they are too few, when a strong following wind makes a cyclist feel as if flying. Racing silent with the wind. At such times the landscape flies by. It seems you are actually gaining on those cars that passed you only moments before. "Good gracious sakes, look at that, Harold! What kind of an Iron Man is that following us? I think that old geezer is actually going to pass us!"

Sweet times, a strong wind aft. Sweet times, life with its blessings.

Passing Cypress Creek Now

Passing the entrance of Cypress Creek campground now, of painful memory. It was here, on my last bike trip before learning I had cancer, that I experienced for the third time in my life the bicyclist's ultimate embarrassment: I fell off my bike.

Upon reflection, there was reason enough for my Cypress Creek fall. Unknown to me, I was carrying that large tumor, and that could have accounted for my puzzling clumsiness, that strange sick feeling.

(The first of my other two falls came when I was in the third grade. The second came just a year ago, during the 1990 "Tour de Toad" bike ride, part of Conway's annual Toad Suck Daze celebration. On both of those occasions, however, I was riding with a pretty girl, so that probably explains that.)

You see them first in your little rearview bike mirror. Those log trucks. Gravel trucks. "Suspicious" vans, pickups, cars. Small, at first glance. Silent. Mysterious. Their sound soon arriving. "Is this the one that'll crowd me off the highway?"

Having traveled a few thousand miles by bicycle over Arkansas

highways, throughout more than a dozen years, I've not many com-
plaints about motorists. Most drivers, by far, seem courteous, conscious
of the need for caution when passing a tour-laden cyclist. But it's a fact:
There is no small danger associated with bicycle touring. Put simply,
it's a lot like life. There are dangers. Risks. Uncertainties.

But—how to say it?—these very factors add to the adventure. The
unknown, even the element of risk, adds zest to life; an edge, a tension,
an excitement that safety and comfort cannot afford. I suppose, how-
ever, that the dangers are the principal reasons I choose to travel alone.
I just don't want to expose friends to such perils. But to be totally truth-
ful, I'll have to acknowledge that that's partly an excuse. I enjoy the
solitude of it all. And that's okay, too.

On this trip, though, I'm blest with the best of both worlds, soli-
tude and companionship. At my Petit Jean campsite I am joined for
an evening campfire cookout by my wife and two friends who motored,
as we say, from Conway. I really think they were just curious. They
wanted to see if the stalwart adventurer was—well—actually still alive.

Gonna Take a Sentimental Journey

It's a dandy, this little handlebar radio. I brought it along with
two thoughts in mind: To listen to some golden oldies, as picked up,
just barely, from that wonderful FM station KFFB, 106.1, in Fairfield
Bay. And to catch Gov. Bill Clinton's press conference at which he
announced for the presidency.

Only I forgot to listen to the Gov. I was too busy enjoying the
outdoors in one of Arkansas's great state parks. Bill would understand, I figured. Probably even would have wished he were here
instead of there.

What is it about a radio antenna that holds such fascination, such
mystery, such magic? Before leaving on this adventure, one of my last-
minute touches was to rig an antenna for my little radio. I taped the
thin, plastic-coated copper wire to the bike frame and extended it
upward the length of the flagpole, from which my hunter-orange safety
banner whips delightfully in the wind. Neat.

I've been fascinated by radio antennas ever since, more than fifty
years ago, I set up my first "ham" radio station. It was a tiny, home-

made battery-operated set with which, by Morse code, I communicated with people in mysterious, faraway places like Kansas, Idaho, and—would you believe it—New York City! Later, with more powerful rigs and better (thought not especially more fascinating) antennas, came those really faraway places with such strange-sounding names as The Congo, Johnson Island, and a ship at sea somewhere off the coast of New Zealand.

But now, on State Highway 154 out of Oppelo, with the unmistakable brow of Petit Jean Mountain in view, it's the Andrews Sisters singing about that sentimental journey they're gonna take. It's even better that the signal is weak, that it breaks up now and then. Sort of like the old days. Edward R. Murrow: "This is London calling."

How grand is memory. How marvelous life's mysteries, such as antennas and radios. And people. And, yes, even illness. (Can illness possibly be "grand"?) And, to be sure, how grand the mystery of recovery. Health. Wholeness. Healing.

I pedal along not even minding the gusty headwind that slows my pace.

Celebrate the Temporary

And now the mountain.

Yes—it's still there. The mountain. And now, John-Boy, here you are. At the foot of that long, steep, man-killer east end of Petit Jean Mountain. There ought to be some kind of ceremony, some sort of ritual observed before you and Old Jim tackle it. But that's really not necessary. You've already been through this countless times in your mind.

During chemotherapy you thought of it. The mountain. When, in those grim days you vomited every twenty minutes for six hours straight and, during each four-day chemo session, lost as much as eleven pounds—you thought of it then. The mountain.

You thought of it, The Mountain, when you caught your reflection in mirrors: Face gaunt, body wracked, not a hair on your head, and that "no hope" look in your eyes. But The Mountain was there. And now it's here. But now you've got Paul Matthews' stump-pullin' gear on your side, John!

Let's do it, Old Jim!

Once, nearly a decade ago, a colleague at the Gazette *asked me, after one of my bicycle trips, "Workman, what in the (expletive deleted) does a humanoid think about while riding a bicycle all day long?" I told him that was a good question, but that I had to confess I couldn't remember.*

But now I do remember: There's one thing you do. You celebrate the temporary. That's what you do.

Celebrate the temporary. That's an insight I got from another friend, one who has known no small portion of life's challenges and hardships. He gave me this gift: "We just need to learn how to celebrate the temporary."

Who among us isn't temporary? Who lives forever? Who isn't terminal? And besides, there's even a sense in which death is yet one more grand adventurous journey—perhaps not a bicycle camping trip, to be sure, but an exciting journey nevertheless.

What does a humanoid do all day long on a bicycle trip? You celebrate the temporary, that's what you do.

The Mystery of Healing

Such a mystery is healing. How to explain it?

In my own instance I credit a number of things. Some are more measurable—such as the traditional protocols of surgery, radiation, and chemotherapy. I believed in those treatments as I underwent them, and I believe in them now. But there are other factors, and they are less measurable.

Such as that silent, inexplicable communication from my doctors and other health professionals: An honest caring; a genuineness; an authentic compassion; telegraphed signals of hope. Those unspoken but powerful signals were, I firmly believe, a significant factor in my healing.

Then there are those other intangibles. How, without seeming weird, does one express those factors? A campfire can do it. Or at least it can help the healing process. As can a bicycle trip. And nights in a tent. And the sounds of coyotes calling in the distance as by candlelight you read your adventure book.

But so, too, may one's "magic rocks" and "special objects"—things of beauty that have more soul in them than sense. Is this too weird a suggestion? All such experiences, and such things, can, I am persuaded, be party to the mysterious miracle of healing.

Perhaps I may be understood if I speak of my special objects and my magic rocks. Two of those objects are especially related to my illness, and I treasure them. Both are simple, common objects, yet both have an element of mystery about them. Both were found on sidewalks as I entered different hospitals in different cities.

The first, found on my initial trip to the hospital in Houston, is a small, circular bit of metal, perhaps a button. On one side is what appears to be an oriental symbol, but it may just be a stylized initial in English. But whatever, the object caught my eye. I picked it up and put it in my pocket.

The second object, found as I entered the hospital in Little Rock to begin my year-long chemo treatments, is a small, silvery-plastic, heart-shaped "prize" of the type found in a box of Cracker Jacks. On one side is an oriental symbol—similar to that on the first object—and on the other are the English words "Good Fortune." A pleasant message indeed for one about to enter a hospital.

"Magic" objects? No, I wouldn't say that. But they are, to me, very special objects because of their power as symbols. They are reminders of what to me is a very special thought: There are a lot of "unknowns" in this universe. And a lot of them, I am convinced, have to do with the mystery of healing and wholeness.

So it is, too, with those many small rocks I've collected throughout the years. Not "magic," and not of any monetary value, but treasured because they remind me of special times. Happy times. Good times with loved ones and friends. Places traveled to. Times enjoyed. Healing times. I believe that a healing, of sorts, comes with remembering such times.

The Miracle of Adventure and Fun

I'm convinced that adventure, or something akin to it, can be a significant factor in recovering one's health. I'm convinced that fun, or something akin to it, can be a significant element in healing.

But adventure need not mean a seventy-five-mile bicycle camping trip. There were times during my recovery when adventure meant simply the setting of a goal, however small—shaving; walking through the living room and into the den; later walking half a block, then one block; then riding my bike down the driveway and back; then riding it a few blocks, and then a mile, and so on.

Fun is perhaps not the precise word, but it's close to it. It has to do with the inward sensation—satisfaction—that accompanies the attaining of goals, however small. It has to do with a sense of joy; a sense of accomplishment that, I believe, contributes significantly to healing.

This, too, I learned from cancer: I could remain ill but still be "healed." Healing and physical wellness, I learned, are not necessarily the same thing. Through the many experiences of love expressed to me during my illness I experienced a very special kind of healing—even though I feared, at that time, that I might never be "truly well," physically, ever again.

And now? Well, there are a lot of roads and byways out there to pedal. Lots of trails to hike. Lots of flowers to smell. Lots of loved ones and friends to be with.

And, oh, yes—there's still that sailing voyage to the South Pacific.

And I almost forgot: There's Mt. Everest.

And, oh, yes, again: There's hang-gliding, too.

And . . . .

CHAPTER VII

Landfalls and Discoveries

Land was created to provide a place for steamers to visit.
—Brooks Atkinson (1951)

1

When Robin Chicks Learn to Fly

If all goes as planned, by the time this column is printed my wife and I will be in London. No, not the one in Pope County. That other London. The one you can't drive to from here. The one with the big tower, clock, and bells.

There's a joyous purpose for our trip. We'll be attending the wedding of our youngest son. We'll be gaining a daughter-in-law. In fact, one week from today, at about the early breakfast hour in Arkansas, our wedding should be in progress.

So, next Saturday morning close your eyes and imagine Arkies in London. Razorbacks in the solemnity of Chelsea Old Church. Imagine yours truly properly decked out in high-church clerical duds to assist in the service. Imagine American southern accents echoing through hallowed halls of British ecclesialdom, so to speak.

What a marvelous occasion for us, this wedding! What a sentimental journey. The marriage of the youngest of our four children. Four down and none to go.

Even as I write this at home, with my study window open, I hear a baby robin chirping up a storm from its nest in the redbud tree just outside. Trying to get out of the nest, I suppose. Trying to convince Mama and Papa that it's time to fly. Jumping, stretching to be off on its own.

Poor Papa Robin. Poor Mama Robin. Turn around and all your chicks are gone.

Do you remember, Chuck—(it's Charles now; no budding young opera singer should be called Chuck)—do you remember that bicycle trip we took together almost half your life ago? Just the two of us, from Little Rock to Conway by way of Wye Mountain? I recall one rest stop in particular, atop the mountain. I spread my poncho on the ground, stretched out, closed my eyes, and, transported by cool breezes and summer shade, traveled awhile on other journeys.

I remember thinking then of the day you were born. I remember, even now, thinking of the years ahead for you. Those unseen, unknowable years, and what they might bring. But what I remember most is how, during our journey together, I was overcome not by tiredness but with that marvelous, wonderful, mysterious emotion we humans call joy.

Joy! It's that same feeling I have now as Mom and I pack our gear to fly to London.

(I was, just now, headed in another direction with these words, but whoops—here comes another memory. Better get out of the way.)

I also recall, Chuck, when we drove you "up East" to college, those years ago. I remember—and it still brings a lump to my throat—hearing the university dean tell us misty-eyed parents that there were only two things we could give our children: Roots and wings. I prayed then, and I pray now: God be in the roots; God be in the wings.

(Dang these memories. They just won't quit. In rushes another.)

I also remember that just a few years ago, Chuck, I thought I might not make it to hear you sing on the opera stage; to learn of your plans to sing in distant, romantic places; to one day, perhaps, even be with you in your wedding! When and where would such a grand event be? To be honest, I didn't figure on London—but what a wonderful development.

And now, come next Saturday, Mom and I will be with you and Alex, and her family and friends in Alex's hometown. How grand. How simply and marvelously grand. (I actually think I wrote that last sentence in my best proper English accent!)

No sounds, now, from my little robin in our redbud tree. I think he made it. I'll bet he's flying free! New adventures. New friends. Joyous in the sunlight on this glorious spring morning.

—*Arkansas Democrat-Gazette,* May 30, 1992.

2

A Yank in London Thinks of Home

LONDON—It seems odd to be thousands of miles from home and smack in the middle of things British and yet to spend an inordinate amount of time thinking about America and Americans. Thinking about the U.S.A. Thinking about a nation and its problems, perils, and prospects.

But perhaps it's always easier to contemplate from a distance. To think detached. To look at forests instead of trees. To seek perspective rather than particulars.

And so I suppose that until an airplane plops me back on U.S. soil in a few days, I'll continue to think a lot about America. About presidential politics, integrity in government, social and racial unrest, family values, and so on and on. Perhaps only after I'm home will I be able to think on England, on this historic land, "this sceptered isle, this blessed plot, this realm, this England."

Still, it is a bit of a shame, by Jove, as we say in the mother tongue, to miss the joy at hand. To not enter fully into the moment, where you are. And especially if you happen to be on holiday (I've picked up a phrase or two) in England.

And there is joy aplenty that brings my wife and me here. The wedding of our youngest son! In fact, that event is to occur at the very moment, quite possibly, that you are reading this column—on this very Saturday morning at about the time most Arkansans are having breakfast.

As this is written in London, the wedding is still some few days away, but I can already bring you this prophetic report: The bride was beautiful, the groom was handsome, the respective parents behaved reasonably well and held up admirably. And yours truly, who is to assist in reading the service, did so with impeccable charm, grace, precision, and no small measure of humility. A jolly good show all 'round.

So much for prophecy. Now some reflections on travel.

Although I've journeyed a bit, there's no way I can pose as a world traveler. But I've trekked enough to know that travel does for one what few other experiences can. Travel broadens our horizons. It deepens our experiences. Travel challenges our prejudices. Travel both frightens us and brings us deep joy.

Travel causes us to look without and within at the same time. It enables us to see others and also better see ourselves. And, if we are honest with ourselves, we often find both experiences humbling.

There is, of course, a very real sense in which one can travel widely without ever leaving home. Henry David Thoreau, who "traveled much in Concord," knew this. As did the poet who observed, "There is no frigate like a book to take you lands away."

It occurs that religious faith is, in truth, one of the most profound of all "travel" experiences. Faith invites us to risk the perils of the soul's venture from here to there. Faith challenges us to make friends with our doubts; it invites us to tread the often-perilous path of inquiry.

Religious faith transports us through majestic halls of mystery and miracle, down garden paths of joy and peace, through storms of suffering and pain, and along the wondrous ways of awe, grandeur, and peace. Religious "traveling" moves one from detachment to caring, from complacency to action, from hate to love.

When soon I return to walk my yard, feed my birds, and tinker my bicycle, I'll continue to travel often, if only in my mind. And many of those journeys will bring me back to London. Back to recall this joyous occasion, the acquiring of a wonderful new family in this place so far from Arkansas, U.S.A.

Although our son and his soon-to-be wife will reside for now in the States, it is so very nice to know that they have family, loved ones, friends, and home here also in "this other Eden, this England."

—*Arkansas Democrat-Gazette,* June 6, 1992.

3

On Living in a Large and Small World

RIDGEWOOD, N.J.—It's a paradox that demands repeated reflection, especially in these times: We live in a world that is both very large and very small. The largeness is perhaps our first impression as children. The smallness is perhaps our lasting impression as adults. Both impressions prevail as one travels, as my wife and I have done during the past eighteen days.

As those who've read the previous two columns know—perhaps only too well—we've been to London to attend the wedding of our youngest son. As this is written, we're back in the United States, in New Jersey, home of our oldest son and his family.

It's been a grand trip, and only the limits of space (rather than the constraints of good manners) keep me from telling more about it than you really want to know. But several impressions prevail, and they seem appropriate to our common interests. Herewith some reflections on those impressions.

The world is ever with us. No matter what the focus of one's travels, the world will not go away. Throughout visits in London, Edinburgh, and elsewhere in the United Kingdom, the news of the day was always very much upon us. The Earth Summit; brutal fighting in Sarajevo; crisis within the European Economic Community; American presidential politics; and so on and on. The world just won't stop turning, even for a wedding.

The Earth Summit in Rio de Janeiro was perhaps the major focus of news reports during our eleven days in the U.K. Newspaper and TV accounts repeatedly focused on President Bush's tough talk regarding the proposed treaty—that American jobs be protected at all cost. The perception in London, fair or not, was that the world's most wealthy nation, the symbol of power, affluence, and overconsumption, was not willing to set the moral example required to confront the most urgent issues facing humanity.

Who, if not this country's religious community, will provide the prophetic word for such an attitude, for such a time?

The world frightens us. That impression, perhaps overblown, is strongest with the infrequent traveler. There is a lot to be afraid of in this world. On our next-to-last day in London, a terrorist bomb was exploded in the city. That same day, in north England, a policeman was killed and another seriously wounded in a terrorist-related event.

Later that day, as we rode the subway, our train (and I suspect the entire London railway system) was stopped for fifteen minutes because, as an unseen official on a loudspeaker reported, a "security check" was being conducted at the Sloane Square station. As the minutes passed and a few people began leaving our train, I pointed out to my wife that our next stop was to be Sloane Square, and that we would be the first post-alert train to make that stop. Have a nice ride.

Though the bomb explosion, the shooting, and the subway delay were minor occurrences compared with previous terrorist-related events, the happenings were enough to get the attention of at least one uptight traveler. We live in a dangerous world.

The world challenges faith. Everywhere throughout the world, at all times, faith is in conflict with despair, hope with defeat, love with hate. Three billboards—two seen while walking in London and the third glimpsed from a speeding train en route to Edinburgh—seemed to symbolize the eternal contest.

Two of the billboards promoted appearances by rock music groups, their names reflecting the mood of despair all too widespread: "Dire Straits" and "Faith No More." The third sign, not so bold, but large enough to be read by train passengers traveling at 125 miles per hour: "Have Faith in God."

That final message, above all others, is always the best of gifts as one nears home. The best to receive. The best to give.

—*Arkansas Democrat-Gazette,* June 13, 1992.

4

The Eternal Search for the Perfect Hat

The first time I went to London, about eighteen years ago, I had big plans to buy a hat. One of those dandy little British caps. But I didn't. I was in the city only a few days and didn't have time to shop properly for a cap. Cap shopping is serious business, not to be hastily pursued. So, on my first trip to London, no cap. It was not a happy trip.

On my second trip to London, some four years later, I did in fact get my cap, and a beauty it was. It was me. And it lasted longer than I could have asked, expiring only a few years ago.

So, last year when my wife and I learned we'd be going to London this month for a wedding, the lights went on again. Hot dog, another hat!

Only those addicted to the eternal search for the perfect hat will understand my elation. (This is religion we're talking about here. Top-priority stuff. Though not quite the quest for the Holy Grail, the search for the perfect hat is of similar high order.)

Scotland's Edinburgh would be the place. With three full days to search—while not visiting castles, palaces, churches, and museums and engaging in other secondary activities—I'd surely have time, at long last, to finally discover my perfect hat.

And I did! But it was only after searching long and hard, and it was only on our last day in that marvelous city.

"Try Jenners" was the repeated counsel when merchants were unable to produce the type of hat I described. "That would be a deerstalker, sir," the clerks said. "You're looking for a deerstalker. Try Jenners."

At Jenners, the nice Scotsman said certainly, sir, they had deerstalkers. And indeed they did. Whole racks full. The clerk helped me find just the right hat. A perfect fit. The perfect look. The hat I'd come all the way from the colonies to purchase. My search had ended!

"Ye look grand in this deerstalker, sir. Indeed, ye do," the gentle Scotsman brogued. And indeed I did, even if I say so myself. Admiring my newly hatted self in the mirror, I noted with joy my wife's approving expression.

"How much?" I finally inquired.

"Only sixty, sir, and ye do look handsome indeed, sir."

Although I'm not too sharp on such things, I figured the man was talking British pounds, not American dollars. And I sort of knew that £60 equaled about $110, or more.

Long pause. Deep breath. "Only sixty, huh?" I think is what I said.

While the wheels turned, I took one long, last look in the mirror, turning my head a bit to the right, a bit to the left, fixing the image permanently in memory, knowing full well it'd have to last throughout eternity.

"Yes, I like it," I said. "And you are correct; it's just right. Perfect. But it's just not in my plans to stalk this many deer."

The Scotsman smiled, chuckled, and then laughed in a wonderfully shy way. "Oh, yes—that grand American sense of humor, sir. Do enjoy your visit in our fine city."

It was odd, but I wasn't as crestfallen as I thought I'd be, not getting my hat. It was enough to know that here in Edinburgh, on the second floor of Jenners, just across the avenue from that marvelous monument in memory of Sir Walter Scott, my perfect hat lay on a shelf.

As we exited the grand brass and glass doors of Jenners, I looked up at that stately monument. I knew that for me, at least, the famous tower also would forever mark the site where rests the perfect hat. And I thought this: Perhaps my search was more fruitful than I imagined. What of all those things we humans do not yet possess but know to be real; know to exist; know to be waiting for us?

It goes to an English poet, Robert Browning, to help us here: "Ah, but a man's reach should exceed his grasp, or what's a heaven for?"

—*Arkansas Democrat-Gazette,* June 20, 1992.

5

Of Carpenters, Kings, and Other Things

I think I've about got this figured out. Why Jesus was a carpenter. (These ponderings have occurred at intervals during the last three months as I've been knee-deep in home-improvement projects.)

It probably wasn't the pay that attracted Jesus to the job—at least not if he worked for the same kind of people I do. Or that most of the time he got to work alone and was his own boss, more or less, although that certainly has its attractions. And it surely couldn't have been the hours. Carpentering, at least the way it's done at our house, is a never-ending job. Meaning there's still more to do after you're done.

No, it must have been something else that attracted Jesus to this carpentering business. The wood, maybe? Quite possibly it had something to do with wood. Wood is a joy to work with. Unlike people, wood responds to your directions (most of the time, anyway). Wood doesn't talk back—at least not a lot—and it finishes up nicely (something else that can't always be said of people). How grand, how satisfying, to work with wood.

(But I do puzzle at this: What did Jesus do when he hit his thumb with the hammer? Or when he cut the board too short? Or when he couldn't make all the corners come out square? It's not easy being a carpenter and a holy person at the same time. Ask me about that.)

It's difficult to isolate those words that adequately express the soul of the carpenter's task, but these must be included: Satisfaction, accomplishment, joy. Carpentry has to do with the joy of creating. It has to do with the primal elation associated with fashioning something with your own hands, the good feeling that comes with a job well done—or at least with a job, well . . . done.

Somewhere in all of this is the secret we're looking for, why Jesus was a carpenter. But, surely, some will say, Jesus wasn't a carpenter just because he liked to saw, hammer, and whittle on wood. This is a weighty matter. There has to be more to it than that.

Well, perhaps there is more to it than that (although perhaps there really isn't). Those who want to find deep theological meanings for Jesus being a carpenter can make a strong point for their case. Carpenters create. They build. They make ordinary things—pieces of wood—become extraordinary things, such as fine tables and chairs and serving bowls and all kinds of useful and beautiful things.

Yes, it's easy to think of carpentry as an appropriate work for one hailed as the son of the Creator, the Master Builder. Which brings us somewhere near a point we'd like to make: There's a whole lot of building and creating—repairing, mending, carpentering—that's needed along the way on our journey through life.

Human relations need mending, human community needs shoring up, whether it's among a people long divided by iron curtains, or families torn by strife, or young people whose lives are messed up with drugs, or a society that has lost touch with its essential roots.

Needed: A few willing carpenters. Openings immediately available.

—*Arkansas Gazette*, November 18, 1989.

6

The Blessings of Storeroom Cleaning

You need to be especially gentle with me right now because I'm going through a difficult time in my life. I'm cleaning out my storeroom. Been at it, in fact, for three whole weeks. And it's not a pretty sight. Nor has the chore produced what you'd call an exactly pretty disposition.

It has helped, though, that the task coincided with the Arkansas Billy Graham Crusade. If you've got to spend your days knee-deep in junk, it's good if you can go to church in the evenings.

Storeroom cleaning is an excellent reminder of how helpful,

and how practical, religion can be. For example, the other day when surrounded by ancient stuff—from roof gutters to tire inner tubes and dried-up cans of paint—I recalled Jesse Jackson's insightful comment: "God don't make no junk." God don't need to make no junk; we humans do well enough on our own.

But I must be honest (another prompting from religion). Once I finally get to it, I sort of enjoy—no, I really enjoy—cleaning out old storerooms. I guess that makes me some sort of strange person. But I can't help it, and God knows I'm sorry.

Consider the blessings of storeroom cleaning. There are primal excitements associated with the task—discovery, nostalgia, wonder, anticipation. There are religious dimensions to the undertaking. Ultimate decisions await. One may be a judge who condemns or a savior who redeems. And if all that is too esoteric, there's the simple joy of accomplishment. There's the sweet satisfaction of having done, at long last, something you knew you should have done months or even years before.

By now you've probably been inspired to get up and start cleaning your own storeroom, so here are some surefire tips:

Tip 1: Make three piles: (1) things to keep; (2) things to throw away; and (3) undecided.

Be prepared to discover that most of the items you uncover will meet the basic requirements for Pile No. 1—too good to throw away but not quite good enough to use right now.

(By midweek, my Pile No. 1 was, of course, by far the largest, containing perhaps fifty or more items. Pile No. 2 consisted of about a half dozen or fewer items, and Pile No. 3 had about four items. By the end of the second week, most of the items in Pile No. 3 had been moved to Pile No. 1—properly dusted and cleaned, of course. You can rationalize keeping most of the stuff by knowing that it'll be cleaned and neatly arranged—at least until the next time you have to search for something in the stack.)

Tip 2: Always get a good night's sleep and a stout breakfast before beginning a fun-filled day of storeroom cleaning. (If you are going to church that evening it's probably wise to take an afternoon nap.)

Tip 3: When your task is complete, brag about it. This is a significant event in your life, and you're due special treatment.

Now—there are bunches of dandy religious lessons hidden away in this storeroom-cleaning image. But I've run out of space, so you'll have to dig them out for yourself. Have fun.

—*Arkansas Gazette,* October 7, 1989.

7

Celebrating the Discovery of Fire

I can't help this, so don't blame me. Blame the calendar. And the weather. I'm talking about yet another one of those annual rituals—or what for me, at least, has become an annual ritual: Preparing the first fireplace fire of the season. ("You see, Mabel, there he goes again. I told you this man was off his rocker.")

But say what you will, the first fireplace fire of autumn is an event that demands its due and proper ritual. As does the arrival of spring, with its first offering of color. As does the birth of a child. And the marriage of lovers. And the burial of a loved one. And a host of other momentous events of life. They each and all are worthy of ritual.

Ritual! Be it high or low or be it done in a steepled sanctuary or on a mountain peak or by the seashore—or before an expectant and eager fireplace—ritual is one of the often unrecognized but absolute essentials of life. Life without ritual is like the heart without a beat; like lungs without air; like the voice without a song.

Without ritual we are so much, so very much, the poorer; if, indeed, we are alive at all. Take away ritual and life is robbed of one of its truly vital elements. Ritual is the way we acknowledge the unspeakable. It is how we pay tribute to the inexpressible. Whether it's football fans shouting Whooo Pig, Sooie! or worshipers lifting silent or spoken petitions before an altar, ritual does for us that which may be done by no other function.

Take ritual from religion and what you have left is cold, austere, lifeless logic and reason—not faith. Ritual, whether a simple prayer or an elaborate ceremony, enables the worshiping individual and community to acknowledge and celebrate some of the most significant elements of faith: Wonder, awe, mystery, adoration, and praise.

But we were talking about fireplaces and the coming of fall and the aroma of wood smoke blessing our neighborhoods. Yes! And surely such a time is worthy of at least a bit of ritual. At any rate I hope so because I'm guilty of such.

My first fireplace fire of the season was celebrated about two weeks ago on one of those first chilly evenings before summer decided to try it again. My first-fire ritual, as observed annually in recent years, included the following: "Special" wood (some would call it scraps) associated with past times, both happy and sad. Kindling shaved from a pinion pine knot picked up while on a family camping trip years ago in the Colorado Rockies. With each shaving the ancient aroma is released anew, evoking memories of happy times and high mountain passes, snow-capped peaks, and chilly winds buffeting our little tent.

The first fire is ignited not by matches but by flint and steel, an attempted tribute to eternal elements and their Maker.

As is the effect with all authentically "ritualed" events, a wood fire can become more than it is. It becomes a joy to the heart, a catalyst to the mind, a nourishment to the soul. Surely such gifts are worth at least a bit of ritual. And surely a child, of whatever age, shouldn't be denied such a joy.

—*Arkansas Gazette,* October 5, 1991.

CHAPTER VIII

Road Hazards and Detours

Danger and delight grow on one stalk.
—English proverb

1

Of Politics, Summer, and Religion

What you need to do, friend, is to get your mind totally off politics before it becomes everlastingly too late. That's where we come in. Such, for the moment at least, is our sole mission in life.

If you'll look at your calendar you'll notice that it's June already. "Good gracious," I hear you saying, "you mean it's actually June already? Whatever happened to May? And April? And all those other months?"

Gone with the wind, like the rest of the hoary past, never to come 'round again.

So here we are, just a couple of weeks away from summer 1990. If you're like me, you can hardly believe it. And hardly wait. I'll bet that you, too, are already thinking summer thoughts. Long, lazy, hazy, crazy summer thoughts. Iced tea with mint and lemon and lots of sugar. Potato salad. Fresh-mowed lawns.

Lawn chairs and long, peaceful summer evenings sparkled by lightning bugs, caressed by the delicious aroma of honeysuckle, enchanted by multitudes of marvelously mysterious night sounds. Vacations. No school. Bare feet. Swimmin' holes. (I may even get to buy a brand-new swimsuit this season since mine has a hole in the knee.)

Ah, summer. Sure, there are mosquitoes and chiggers and crawling things, but so what. That's the way it is with summer, wonderful summer. Summer! Let 'er come.

But you do realize, of course, that you don't get off scot-free during summer. I mean, life does go on. And that means responsibilities. Like, for instance—and pardon me for bringing this up again when I all but promised not to—even though we've finally gotten those primary elections behind us, we aren't home free.

Yes, there's that general election still to come in November. That means we've got to survive some more campaigning. But perhaps that's just as well. A too-sudden withdrawal from that kind of diet—

which, it seems, we've been subjected to constantly for the past hundred years or so—could be perilous.

But, anyway, somewhere in the midst of all this summertime politics and such is where religion comes in. Truth to tell, good religion and good politics have a lot in common. Both, at their highest and finest, are concerned with ideals, values, and responsibilities.

Both, at their best, are committed to the welfare of the human family, the preservation of the environment, and the fulfillment of solemn duties to generations yet to come. Yes, our election process has some problems, such as the preponderance of negative, mean-spirited campaigning that destroys integrity and evades real issues and does perhaps more damage to the fragile social fabric than can be measured.

So here's a suggested addition to your 1990 summertime agenda: Ponder, meditate, and perhaps even pray about how we all may become better stewards of a good but flawed political process.

—*Arkansas Gazette,* June 2, 1990.

2

An Open Letter to Governor Bill Clinton

This being my last chance before the Democratic National Convention to mix religion and politics, I suppose I'd better get with it. Since it's always sort of fun to read other people's mail, I'll do this in the form of an open letter. Herewith is such a letter to Arkansas governor Bill Clinton.

Dear Bill:

I know that I'm pretty excited by all this—our own governor poised as the Democrat's likely nominee for president of the United States!—and so I can only imagine what you must be feeling these days. And what a tangled mix of emotions it must be!

Imagine: Unless something totally unforeseen occurs in the next several days, what seemed an outside chance just a few short months ago is now about to become a reality. It's almost too much to take in. But you don't need me to tell you that.

Indeed, I suspect that swarms of people are trying to get your ear these days—advisors, party strategists, friends, well-wishers, opponents; people with axes to grind, agendas to promote, old and new political debts to pay, and so on and on. Gracious, it must be terribly difficult, even if exciting, to be Bill Clinton this week.

What someone once said about this country could perhaps be said about a probable nominee for president: "What this probable nominee needs is fewer people telling him what this probable nominee needs."

But having said that, let me lay on you yet even a few more suggestions about what a probable nominee might ponder during these fateful countdown hours before Bill Clinton of Arkansas stands front and center in the nation's spotlight.

First, don't forget what you learned in Sunday school. Especially don't forget those things you learned about values, principles, integrity, truth, and the radical demands of love.

And don't forget the message of those staunch Baptist preachers, those crusty old prophets who held that religious liberty is a thing of such rare value that it dare not be fiddled with by government; and that the free democratic state is of such value that it dare not yield to the subtle courtings of any single religion.

Second, don't pull your prophetic punches. Don't be afraid to challenge us with those lofty ideals that are our greatest national heritage, our truest treasure. Remind us who we are and from whence we have come. Tell us, in no uncertain terms, what marvels are freedom, justice, equality before the law, equal opportunity, and the rights of a democracy.

Tell us, without equivocation, what terrible things are bigotry, racism, unbridled greed, and unequal privilege. Remind us that in this land of the free many are still enslaved by powerlessness, poverty, sexism, and other modern forms of bondage.

Third, remind us wherein lies our authentic greatness. Tell us that what makes a nation great is not its military might nor its economic strength, but its values, its ideals, its visions, and dreams. Tell us that a nation's true worth lies in the essential goodness of its people and not in its wealth, power, or privilege. Tell us that a nation conceived in liberty and dedicated to the proposition that all are created equal may never rest so long as injustice remains.

Tell us that wrong is wrong and right is right, and that it is our common duty always to distinguish between the two.

Bill, I've long believed that one day you could make our nation a good president. Perhaps even a great one. But more important is that you be a good man. A good husband. A good father. I will be among the many who will be praying for you, and for our country, in these most important days. God bless you.

Sincerely, John.

—*Arkansas Democrat-Gazette,* July 11, 1992.

3

In Which God Grants an Interview

Meanwhile, back in heaven, the press office finally got around to returning its calls. "Okay, we're ready now. You can do your interview."

"My interview! Honest? No kidding? You're joshin' me!" (That's me, excited.)

"No, we're not kidding, and, yes, you can do your interview. We figured that since you're sort of retired and not much of a real journalist anyway, you'd be safe. So hang on. God'll be on the phone in a moment. He-She—that's what we call God during election years—is on another line."

I couldn't believe it. All these months leading up to the New Hampshire primaries I'd been trying to get an interview with God, to see how God was feeling about all this. But I never could get through. The lines were always jammed. Once, though, God actually did pick up the phone, but we were interrupted by a call-waiting signal and I got put on hold. After a couple of weeks of holding, I sensed that God wasn't overly excited about talking with me, so I hung up and went back to painting my closet. That sort of bothered me, though, hanging up on God. I hope I didn't mess up big.

But anyway, there I was, actually talking to heaven's press office, though now getting a recorded message: "Please continue to hold. Your call is important to us and it will be processed next."

My questions! I almost panicked. I couldn't remember my questions. I'd have to wing it.

"Yes? How may I help you?"

(That voice! Nothing like I'd ever imagined. A Yankee accent.)

I froze. "Yes? Are you there?" That voice again.

"Yes, Sir. Ma'am. I am. I'm here. And please pardon my hesitation. I'm a bit nervous."

"First question, please."

"Yes. First question. Well, could you tell me, please, who you voted for in the New Hampshire primaries?"

"Love one another."

"Sir? Ma'am?"

"Love one another."

"Oh. Well. I'm not sure I understand. Did you answer my question?"

"Yes. Next question, please. And, John, get with the program."

"Certainly, Sir. Ma'am. Let's see. What do you believe about all the carrying on—the bickering, half-truths, untruths, scheming, plotting, and all that stuff—that goes on in politics?"

"Love one another."

"Oh. Thank you."

"Any more questions?"

"Yes, Sir. Ma'am. I was just wondering, if it's not asking too much, could you please tell me who's going to be the next president of the United States?"

"Love one another."

(Pause.)

"Now just a dadgum minute, God! [I was getting bolder.] I know that you're God and that I'm just the interviewer and that you've got bunches of calls waiting, but you're not answering my questions! Why, we've got folks who write for this newspaper, including myself, who've got better answers than you've given, if you'll excuse my abruptness."

"Love one another, Workman. You want I should draw you a picture?"

"But Sir. Ma'am. What kind of answer is that? You've not even listened to my questions! Can't you understand simple questions?"

"Look, John-Boy. Maybe, just maybe, it's not my answers that aren't making sense. It just might be your silly questions. That's the trouble with you humans—you never could get the questions right. Think about it. When you get the questions right, call back."

—*Arkansas Democrat-Gazette,* February 22, 1992.

4

The Truth About Character Flaws

Yes, Virginia, it's true, though it's painful to acknowledge: Bill Clinton has a character flaw. Bunches of people have whispered it of late, and you're bound to have heard. More than whispered, actually. People shouted it. People talking politics, if you can imagine such a thing.

But whatever, I'm here to confirm the sad news: Bill Clinton, Baptist, does in fact have a character flaw. But, Virginia—and this is difficult to report, but you're old enough now to hear it—so, too, does George Bush have a character flaw. Yes, I'm bold enough to declare it right here in print: None other than President of the United States George Herbert Walker Bush, Episcopalian, has a character flaw. And you can tell him I said so.

And as long as we're at this, Virginia, I suppose I might as well tell the whole truth: Even I, your sainted friend—a Methodist!—have a character flaw, itsy-bitsy though it certainly must be.

There's more, too. Not only do all of us mentioned here have CFs, but so, too—brace yourself for this, Virginia, it's almost more than I can say—so, too, do you, however tiny that flaw must surely be.

How, you ask, do I know all this secret stuff? Well, Virginia, it's because I'm in the religion business, and this is the kind of inside information that goes with our territory. We religion professionals know all about these things. Character flaws. That's what we do—

we deal in character flaws. All day long. Around the clock. And, believe you me, it's not especially fun, this CF business.

But, anyway, if this were the end of the story, Virginia, I'd get out of the CF business. But there is, thank goodness, some really good news for all of us who are plagued with CFs. (Some people call CF "original sin," but I can't figure out why. I always thought original sin was a sin I thought up all by myself.)

This good news? It's been called, and I like this term, *original blessing,* and it reveals some dandy truths about us humans and about our Creator. Granted that all of us mortals just might be tainted with character flaws, we're also endowed with this marvelous gift of original blessing.

So, when I think of Bill Clinton's character flaws—and George Bush's, and my own, and even yours, Virginia—I also ponder and marvel at the original blessing with which we've been endowed. Our potential. Our possibilities. Our character assets. Our possibilities for change.

You see, Virginia, I don't lose a lot of sleep over this character flaw business. I choose, rather, to celebrate this other truth about life, and it is a grand truth indeed: The Creator is in the redemption business. The blessing business. The Creator stays awake nights offering us a hand-up from our character flaws. Our Creator is in the saving business, if you please. Offering to rescue you and me— and Bill and George and everyone else—from our character flaws. Giving second chances. Even third—and seventieth chances or more, if need be.

What can save us from our character flaws? Love. Only love.

Just think, Virginia: What if there were little groups of people out there who could love us out of our character flaws? That'd be pretty neat, wouldn't it. But I suppose that's too much to expect. I guess we'll all just have to go on fussing and fighting with each other. Politics as usual.

But still, it'd be great if only there were some ways we could help each other overcome these pesky character flaws. Got any ideas, Virginia?

—*Arkansas Democrat-Gazette,* October 24, 1992.

5

Of Doves and Geese and Ways to Peace

For Noah, it was a dove. A single, solitary dove. For me it was a bunch of Canadian geese, possibly a hundred or more, high above the Hendrix College campus in Conway.

They honked, my geese did—no, they trumpeted—their way north, passing over the college chapel, my destination last Sunday evening to attend a vigil for peace in the Middle East. Once beyond the chapel, the marvelous winged creatures hesitated, reset their compasses, hooted directions to each other, and turned west.

They were bound, I figured, for the wildlife refuge at Holla Bend, a favored spot for goose peace vigils and prayer meetings, that sort of thing. Sniffing the air for olive branches, I supposed.

Birds and animals, I thought—as well as humans—have high stakes riding on this present world crisis. A sign of peace, my geese? A sign of promise? Or perhaps a sign of grim happenings ahead? I wondered. At any rate, who wouldn't head for refuge on this damp, chilly evening a few days before a line drawn in the sand of a distant desert is scheduled to be crossed? Where indeed is refuge to the discovered in such a moment? Where, and in what, is peace to be found? And where is peace not to be found?

The ancient questions seem almost moot on this third morning after one of the most massive air attacks in history. War has, in fact, come. Were our prayers for naught? Did our vigils fail?

Those dumb geese. How can one dove be smarter than one hundred geese?

The age-old questions remain. Perhaps the latter question—where is peace *not* to be found—is more in need of immediate attention.

Item: Peace is never to be found in vain face-saving. How sad, how truly sad—no, how insane—that we just might have come to this grim moment in history primarily because the leaders of two nations, facing a hastily imposed deadline, must save face. Too harsh an indictment? Unfair? Too simplistic? I think not. Which is more noble, more just, more humane, more truly patriotic: To save face or to save lives?

Item: Peace is never secured through military might. That's an old proposition, often stated but all too frequently ignored. Throughout our history we've boasted that a nation's true strength is not in might but in right. Long have we claimed that our greatest strength is not in our vast military power, but in our ideals, our principles—freedom, justice, equality, opportunity, democracy, brotherhood.

An early observer said it: "America is great because it is good. If America ceases to be good, it will cease to be great."

Item: Peace is not to be found in self-serving and shortsighted policies clothed in morality-laden rhetoric that reeks of hypocrisy.

Isn't that kind of talk unpatriotic? Isn't it a betrayal of our fighting men and women in Operation Desert Storm? No, it is not. It's an effort at truth, a vital foundation for peace. Certainly we must support our young men and women in the Persian Gulf. But we do that best by being makers of peace, not boosters of an unnecessary war.

Where, then, may peace be found? Where else than in those ancient tenets honored by the world's great religions—including Christianity, Islam, and Judaism, the religions held dear by so many citizens of the very nations now at war.

No more blood for oil. No more blood for face-saving. No more blood for an unnecessary war.

—*Arkansas Gazette,* January 19, 1991.

6

Kicking the War Habit

That's the trouble with war. You get hooked on it. It's not easy to let go of a good war. Especially a popular war, one you've won so overwhelmingly, so quickly, so easily. Letting go of war is sort of like giving up on whiskey or gambling or chocolate. Once you're addicted, it's tough to kick the habit.

At least that's the case with short and successful wars. At least as long as the casualties don't hit home. When the casualties do hit home, then that's another matter indeed. Then you're the one who's been gotten ahold of, and in a tragic way. Then war won't ever let you go.

For seven months now we've enjoyed such a steady diet of the exhilaration of impending and real war that now that it's over we're experiencing the pangs of withdrawal. War, especially the way it's packaged and sold today, is heady and habit-forming entertainment: Multiple daily press briefings by charismatic military commanders; the mesmerism of high-tech killing machines; the infectious camaraderie of patriotism; persuasive leaders assuring us our cause is just and endorsed by none other than God himself. An orgy of chauvinism and jingoism offered as patriotism. It's little wonder this war was so popular among Americans.

But alas comes a reckoning.

During wartime one learns, or is reminded of, some harsh truths about oneself. I'll illustrate with myself. In recent weeks I've been reminded that there's a part of me—dare I confess it?—that enjoys war. It's a fact, a deeply disturbing fact that I confess with shame.

It's the little boy in me that never completely gave up his toy pistols and rubber-gun rifles. The little boy who never felt as big as when playing war in the backyard of the Methodist parsonage in Fayetteville, Arkansas (with the Baptist preacher's son among "the enemy"). War was great fun and we fought it religiously.

A part of me relived that same "fun" recently in watching daily episodes of this edited-for-TV war. Again, I'm shamed by the confession, but it's true. As a clergyman I've devoted my adult life to what I believe is one way we may overcome such base tendencies within us humans.

A wise person who knew this dark truth about us observed long ago that humanity needs "a moral equivalent of war." Think about that: A moral equivalent of war. Is it possible that such activities as peacemaking, working for justice, and trying to save the planet could be as exhilarating and as "enjoyable" as war?

Is it possible that our battles against drugs, poverty, racism, bigotry, ruinous national deficits, AIDS, teenage pregnancy, suicide, ignorance, unemployment, and other social ills could be waged with the same excitement as "real war"? Is it possible that we humans could be as smart, crafty, bold, and courageous in fighting social ills as in fighting each other?

Those are urgent questions rightly addressed to every patriotic American.

The hard work of peace has begun in the Persian Gulf and the Middle East. An equally hard work—combating society's ills—awaits at home. Will we be as gung ho in working for social justice as we've been in fighting, and enjoying, our shooting wars?

—*Arkansas Gazette,* March 9, 1991.

7

Another Spy in from the Cold

I don't particularly want to do this, but I sort of can't help it. All this talk about homecoming celebrations for our Desert Storm troops has caused me to do some remembering, or at least to try to do some remembering. About my own homecoming from what was left of World War II by the time I was discharged from the army.

I'll not mention that I spent considerably more time overseas than have our Desert Storm fighters. I'll not mention that I came excitingly close to being immortalized as the last casualty of World War II, even though the war had been over for several months.

(That was on Iwo Jima and had to do with Japanese soldiers who were hiding in caves, unaware they were supposed to quit shooting. But mostly it had to do with an American GI's pet monkey, which one dark night on a jungle trail—just minutes after we greenhorns, on a brief transit stop on the island, had been warned of such a danger—jumped on my back and grabbed me around the neck, almost scaring me to death on the spot. An ignoble fate narrowly escaped.)

Nor will I go into detail about what I did in the service, mostly in Korea. Only that I was, in fact, a—well, a spy. For our side.

There are long and detailed descriptions of what I did, but if I told you all that I'd have to kill you. (That's a joke, the kind we spies used to enjoy telling.) What we did—I was one of only eight such persons in the army's Pacific Theater—had to do with getting our country ready for its next war, which we did, in fact, finally get around to fighting.

Uncle Sam thought so highly of what we eight men did that we had the No. 1 priority for evacuation in the event of hostilities. There's still more, but if I told it I'd have to kill you again. (Same joke.)

But back to my homecoming. I don't remember much about my homecoming other than I got seasick on the troopship and that my mom and dad and two brothers and my Sunday school teacher and a fellow I owed twenty-five dollars all said they sure were glad to see me again, and I said, "me too."

But no yellow ribbons. No big celebrations. No hoopla. And gratefully nobody tried to politicize our homecoming. I had done my job. I was a good spy. I served my country well.

But those were simpler times. Issues were clear. Right was right and wrong was wrong. Or at least it seemed that way. And I was young, enamored with my job and not overly burdened with whatever moral issues might have been involved in it all. Such irritations were to come later, and they did—the weightiness of morality; the stickiness of ethics; the pickiness of do-right rules. Which brings me to the present.

The current issue, it seems, has to do with patriotism. With what patriotism is, with what it isn't, and with what it means.

Why is there something uncomfortable about all this hoopla? The answers aren't easy to identify, but they have something to do with patriotism being "used." Patriotism being politicized. Cashed in on. Devalued.

Are there somewhere groups of people that could help this troubled family of nations, poised on the frontier of a new world order, discover an honorable patriotism? A patriotism that could save us all, together? A patriotism that would please our common Creator?

—*Arkansas Gazette*, May 4, 1991.

CHAPTER IX

Rest Stops

Consider the lilies of the field, how they grow. . . .
—The Gospel of Matthew 6:28

1

Random Thoughts While Garden Walking

What a marvelous sentiment. What a wonderful memorial. That brief but thought-provoking sentence, etched in a small granite plaque in a garden walkway on the campus of Hendrix College in Conway. The plaque honors the memory of longtime faculty member Dr. Tom Clark, now deceased almost two years.

Placed by the family and the college grounds committee, the six-inch square honors the biology professor who was instrumental in numerous campus beautification projects throughout nearly three decades.

"The garden you gave us continues."

As would befit the unassuming professor, there are no other words on the plaque. No name. No date. No memorial inscription. The square, which features a single marigold etched into the stone, is inconspicuous among the thousands of lookalike bricks in the shaded walkway near the Trieschmann Fine Arts Building. The simple statement will give its silent testimony for generations to come. The simplicity is appropriate. For although this is indeed a memorial to a grand and gentle person—a husband, father, loved one, teacher, and friend to many—it also is a monument to a profound truth. A truth about the wonder and magic of a gift. A truth about giving. A truth about receiving. A truth about gardening, and garden tending, as metaphors for life. In short, a truth about love.

One can imagine a scene decades into the future: A hurried student, late for class, catches something out of the corner of an eye. "What's this? One of these tiles is different." Retracing steps, the student will read the inscription: "The garden you gave us continues."

"Hmmm," this student may ponder, "I wonder what that's all about."

Perhaps such a brief encounter will cause the student, as such an encounter has caused this writer, to ponder a grand truth: Each of us has been enriched by gardens others have planted and others have tended; gardens that we, in turn, are to tend for others yet to come.

As do all authentic memorials, this simple six-word inscription evokes emotions from deep within. Gratitude. Wonder. Joy. Peace.

Such emotions and thoughts are especially appropriate in this Lenten season. And doubly so on this last weekend before Holy Week, the time when Christians recall major events in the life of Jesus. For Christians, Holy Week is a time of remembering our Lord's pain, sorrow, grief, and, yes, apparent defeat. But as with our own lives, all of that is part of the garden, part of the gift.

Christians also know that Holy Week is prelude. Prelude to Easter. Prelude to joy. "The garden you gave us continues."

So many, the gardens!

Garden-walking is, by nature, essentially a personal experience, so I must speak personally. A day never passes that I do not think of the principal garden-givers in my life—my parents, family, and friends. This very week, while rummaging through some old family things, I happened upon a small object, a solid brass bell, that opened the floodgates of memory. I recalled stories of how my Uncle George and Aunt Liza, missionaries in China and later in India, brought us this bell from a temple in the remote highlands of China. Unless my memory is overenriched, I recall that temple being within sight of the vast, towering Himalaya Mountains. How grand an image.

For a moment I held the little bell, unrung I suspect for decades. Then, with its first gentle, crystal-clear "ting"—a high-pitched, echoing, ice-blue sound—memories of happy family times swept over me. A flower in the garden.

And so, Tom, George, Liza, and all of you other grand gardeners and gifters, hear this chime: The many gardens you gave us continue.

—*Arkansas Democrat-Gazette*, April 11, 1992.

2

On Watching Young Dogwoods Grow

We planted them a few weeks ago, three young dogwood trees, and I believe they're going to make it. They look good. Our trees' former home is a beautiful wooded hillside near Toad Suck Lock and Dam west of Conway, where our friends have a lovely home overlooking the Arkansas River.

Although our young trees couldn't actually see the river from their rustic neighborhood—the river is over the ridge and down the hill—they certainly must have known that it was there, that ancient bringer of life, that river of many waters. Surely they knew it was flowing, sometimes gently, sometimes mightily.

And though shaded by older, taller, and more experienced forest dwellers, our young trees knew that those other givers of life—the sun, the soil, and the air—also were faithful in bearing their mysterious, magic gifts. And now, in their new home, our little trees are greeted daily by those same life-givers. The same sun warms them by day. The same moon brightens their nights. The same air breathes its secrets into their veins. And the same water, though perhaps a cousin of that which flows near their former home, also is present to silently nurture and sustain their young lives.

It's all working. Signs of life are everywhere. Small limbs, barren and brittle only weeks ago, now are softening, swelling, taking on the color and velvety feel of life. Tiny buds are emerging, however slowly. There is life and growth here, and the message is clear: There's more, so very much more, to come.

Before transplanting our new little trees we carefully selected the site for each. Two would be in our backyard, where they could be enjoyed from our patio and seen through our den windows. The other would be in our front yard, for passersby to enjoy and where we could catch glimpses of it from our living room and from my study.

Although I'm reluctant to reveal this, I suppose I should tell you about the brief ritual—some would call it strange if not worse—I conducted before introducing each fragile tree to its new home. I spoke gently to each tree. I lifted each toward the sky, and then— I really don't know why—I momentarily held each, in turn, toward the four points of the compass, north, south, east, and west, as though to reorient it to friends and forces in places far and near.

Weird? Perhaps. But this ritual was more for my benefit than that of the trees. It was to remind me, at that appropriate moment, of some very basic realities we humans take so for granted: The interrelatedness of all life, be it vegetable, mineral, or animal, and our dependence as humans not only on God but also on all creation.

A bit unusual, you say? Maybe. But if God is one and life is whole, we've got a lot of kin out there. Have you hugged your trees today?

—*Arkansas Gazette,* March 3, 1990.

3

The Joys and Pains of Being Different

It's my favorite comment of the week and one of the nicest things ever said about me. A genuine compliment. My wife and I, riding our bicycles in the neighborhood on a springlike afternoon, saw friends in their front yard and stopped to visit.

Me, on my old touring bike, heavy laden with travel gear, survival equipment, handlebar pack, luggage rack, custom touring bars with angry-dog spray bottle attached, map holder, two water bottles, tall flexible flagpole aft with tattered orange flag flapping. Me, in my silly self-created bike helmet with custom sun visor, etc. Me, ever ready for the open road. Me, the look of distant horizons chiseled all over my rugged countenance.

By contrast, my lovely wife is fashionably attired in a colorful outfit, an up-to-date ladies bike helmet, matching gloves, and so on.

Our friend, speaking to her elementary school daughter: "Look,

Rebecca. See Mr. Workman? You should never be afraid to be different."

How wonderful! How wise a thing for a parent to say to a child. And how nice a thing to be said about me, though I'm not at all sure I'm worthy of such a high compliment.

I've thought a lot about that casual remark. "Never be afraid to be different." It may be stretching things a bit, but the remark has wide application. For instance, it's sort of like something Jesus once said to his disciples. "Look, fellas," Jesus said (this is the Very Revised Version), "you're supposed to be *in* the world but not *of* the world. Get it? You should never be afraid to be different." Or something like that.

Never be afraid to be different. Like a lot of good religious advice, that's easier said than done. It's not easy being different. (Ask Kermit the Frog.) Most of us like to be liked. And when you're different—when your mother dresses you funny—it's not easy to be liked. Ask any of us teenagers.

It's never easy and it's certainly never a whole lot of fun to stand out from the crowd. But for religious groups, at least for those patterned after the biblical example, being different goes with the territory.

It's what we do, being different. It's who we are. Different. When the world gets on the bandwagon for war, we are to be different. We are to be peacemakers. When the world forgets the fundamental lessons of love, we are to be different. We are to be lovers. When the world becomes consumed with hate, violence, and revenge, we are to be different. We are to be reconcilers.

No, it's not always easy to sort out the issues. Aggressors must be restrained. Evil must be resisted. Wrong must be stood up to. Injustice must be put down, sometimes at great cost. But when such heavy realities arise, the biblical religions are well counseled to remember who they are. And what they are. And how it is they are to do the difficult, complex, agonizing business of peacemaking.

"Look, little children. Never be afraid to be different." After all, that's what you're supposed to be. Different.

—*Arkansas Gazette,* February 16, 1991.

4

Life Through a Rearview Mirror

You really need to see this. I've got what is probably the only desk in Arkansas—maybe even in the whole world—that comes complete with rearview mirrors. Two of them. Actually, they're side-view mirrors. They enable me, while seated at my computer, to not only look out on God's beautiful world through the window at my left, a westward view, but also to look both north and south along Mitchell Street to see what's happening in those directions, too.

(And, by glancing at yet another mirror that reflects over my right shoulder and through my study door and out the window in our breakfast nook, I can see where the sun rises, though I don't often witness that event. It's nice.)

But about this mirror arrangement. You probably think I ordered all this from a catalog, but I didn't. I made it myself. I even thought it up all by myself.

The four-by-five-inch mirrors, in wood frames, are mounted on swivel joints for easy adjustments. I must say I'm rather proud of this project, devised and constructed from special space-age materials—wooden ball joints whittled from pieces of scrap pine and inserted into what we in the desk rearview mirror trade call "special flexible cylindrical sockets"—in fact pieces of old car radiator hose. (Don't ever throw anything away.)

Both of these identical units—vision modules, we call them—are painted a delicate antique white to match the window frame. This is no junky deal we're talking about. There are other neat things about my desk, but this is probably all you can handle just now. Besides, we've got to sermonize.

Today's lesson is about looking at life. About trying to see, to feel, to experience all that one possibly can that life and the Creator have to offer. Such an undertaking is a worthy endeavor indeed, worth whatever trouble and expense it might take—even building rearview mirrors.

(My mirrors cost me $1.49 apiece at Fred's. But what the heck, it was worth the investment.)

Let me count the ways my mirrors brighten my life.

In my north-view mirror I can see the beautiful dogwood trees at the neighbor's house on the corner of Mitchell and Prince Streets. And there's the Episcopal Church, an ever-lovely reminder of lofty things to think upon. In my south mirror I can see the roses on our front fence, the bright and colorful azaleas in the next block, the traffic on Caldwell Street, giant oak trees, and my mailman when he brings all my personal third-class mail each morning.

The fact is, of course, that as handy and dandy as desk mirrors are, they really aren't absolutely essential for getting the best look at life. Several things do that better. Religious faith—including its mystery, wonder, and awe and the commitment it entails—is one such help. Another is healthy doubt, the kind that provokes curiosity, which leads to inquiry, which in turn can lead to discovery and reverence.

Wonderful mirrors, all.

But if you still want your desk rigged with personalized side-view mirrors, you need to hire a consultant. A really good one. A high-priced consultant. We could probably think of somebody.

—*Arkansas Gazette,* April 21, 1990.

5

This Confession Good for the Sole

I suppose I ought to confess it: One of the things I enjoy most about being retired is getting to wear white socks. Every day. Except, of course, on Sundays. I'm told that white socks don't look quite right with my dark blue church suit. I don't know why—they look okay to me.

Ah, white socks. Ah, cotton socks. Comfortable, casual, do-what-you-want-to socks. Don't-get-dressed-up-for-nobody socks. Ah, retirement socks.

I can even put up with wearing those uncomfortable synthetic black dress socks for three hours every Sunday because I know that just as soon as I get home from church I can yank them off, put on my comfortable white socks, get back into my cozy retirement duds, and become my true self again.

Ah, comfort. Ah, casualness. What is it about old clothes that make us so comfortable? I really don't know, but maybe it has something to do with the shucking of pretense; with being authentic; with the discarding of show; with the enjoyment of naturalness. But perhaps that's making too much a case for old clothes and cotton socks. On the other hand, perhaps not.

Anyway, while speaking of clothes, I suppose there's another confession I ought to make, and it's one that scares me: I'm actually beginning to like some of these fashionable contemporary colors and styles. And that, I fear, is a bad sign.

I'm afraid it's an omen written about by the *Gazette*'s really old columnist, Bob Sells. He wrote that you could spot retired people by the bright green trousers they wear at the shopping malls. I could be headed that way, and it's downright frightening.

Just yesterday, while shopping for hardware items at a local superstore, I found myself browsing through the men's clothing section. I even tried on a dandy jacket, a sporty item in those bright neon colors that have such fancy, trendy names. But I actually liked the way the jacket looked on me. And, although it's probably the kind of garment bought only by teenagers and rap musicians, I've almost worked up enough courage to go back and purchase it. I figure it'd look pretty snazzy with white socks.

I think I can blame these changes in taste, in part anyway, on a telephone call I received a couple of weeks ago at the ungodly hour of 2:00 A.M. Awakened from deep sleep, I picked up the phone and heard those tell-tale dormitory sounds so recognizable in this three-college town. "John?" the youthful voice said. "Yes," I replied, still half asleep. Pause. "Is this John?" "Yes—but which John were you calling?" I mumbled.

"John (somebody)," the young man said. "Well, I'm afraid you've got the wrong John," I told him. Then came this obviously heartfelt apology: "Oh, mannn! Golly, dude, I'm sorry!"

At breakfast the next morning, I told my wife that being awakened at 2:00 A.M. was worth it just to be called "dude."

Well, there's no sermon here yet, but try this: God loves us, just as we are. Even us dudes. Just as we are. Without one plea.

Short sermon today because I've got to rush back to the superstore to get that jacket before some other dude latches on to it.

—*Arkansas Gazette,* October 12, 1991.

6

Things Never to Say to a Violin Player

One of the fun things about having your own newspaper column is you get to tell the whole world cute stories about your grandchildren. And you get to do it without having to listen to all those other grandparents out there who are jumping up and down for equal time.

Our oldest son, reporting from New Jersey, tells the following regarding our five-year-old granddaughter, Julia. You need to know that Julia is taking violin lessons.

The following exchange occurred while the little family—which consists of Mama, Papa, little brother Marcus, and big sister Julia—was enjoying a PBS TV program featuring the renowned violinist Itzhak Perlman—you know, the kind of quiet evening so many of us enjoy so regularly.

Julia to father: "Papa, am I a better violinist than he is?"

Papa, a confessed former trumpet player with good memory, reports he avoided a direct answer but that Julia persisted. Here's from Papa's report: "Finally I said that she played well, but not quite as well as the acknowledged virtuoso Perlman." Papa reported—and it's almost more than a grandfather can bear—that Julia "burst into tears as only a five-year-old can." When her sobbing had mostly subsided, Julia turned and properly educated her father: "Papa, you never say that to a violin player!"

To which this grandfather shouts a hearty amen. I'm with you, Julia. We artists are special, and the sooner these common people learn it the better.

All of which invites us to think religious thoughts. Thoughts such as: What are all those things that one should never say? What are those things that one should say maybe once in a while? And what are those things that one should say lots and lots of times?

Let's take those questions in reverse order. The following is my own list, learned from no small amount of experience, most of it painful. You've probably got your own list. If not, it's time you made one.

Things one should say quite often: Please. Thank you. I love you. I'm sorry. Forgive me. Yes, I did it. No, I didn't do it. Yes, I did it, but I didn't mean to do it, and I won't do it again. When all else fails there's the always dependable, Yes, I did it and God knows I'm sorry.

Things one should say quite seldom: Buzz off. Get lost. Don't bother me. It's none of your business. Yes, I did it and I meant to do it. No, I didn't do it, but I wish I had done it. There's a bunch of other things to seldom say, but perhaps this is enough to give you the general idea. You take it from here.

Things one should never ever say: Never. I quit. No, I won't forgive you. I don't care. It doesn't matter to me. There are, to be sure, whole chapters of things one should never ever say. But space is limited. Make your own list.

While we're at this, let's add another category or two. This is fun.

Things to never say to your preacher: Why, Brother Smith, every sermon you preach is better than the next one! Or: That was a rip-snortin' sermon, preacher! I just wish all them sinners in our church had been present to hear it!

Things preachers should never say to their people: God loves you, and I'm workin' on it. Or: Brother Jones, I'm planning to preach an especially tough sermon on sin next Sunday, and I hope you'll make an extra-added effort to be in attendance.

So what's the point here? Why all this silliness?

There are things we need to hear that are hard for us to hear. And there are things we need to say that are hard for us to say. Perhaps this guideline can help: Let us say what we say, and let us hear what we hear, in love.

—*Arkansas Democrat-Gazette,* April 4, 1992.

7

Life Lessons from Three Plucky Friends

I'd like to introduce to you three of my friends. Three relatively new friends. Three small friends from whom I've relearned large lessons for life. I want you to know Peggy, Bobby, and Spunky.

In order for you to really know my friends I must report some biographical data. And I must tell you their full names, names by which these friends have become part of my life.

First, meet Peggy. Peggy the Peg-Legged Grackle. Peggy, with whom I've visited off and on during the past couple of years. Peggy first appeared one fall morning with a bunch of grackles who'd come to scavenge around our birdfeeder. But unlike her chums, Peggy limped along the outskirts, doing her best to salvage a morsel or two.

It was obvious: Peggy was lame. She apparently had suffered a severe injury to one leg. On a return visit, Peggy appeared so handicapped that she'd be easy prey for the neighborhood cat. I picked her up and placed her high in a bush. She remained in the area for a few days and then was gone. In the months and years that followed, Peggy would occasionally show up at our feeder. I saw her most recently just a couple of weeks ago.

Peggy, of silent witness to the indomitable will to live.

And now meet Bobby. Bobby the Bobtailed Cardinal. Bobby—what a delight! When Bobby first showed up at our feeder I thought I was seeing things. What's this? A cardinal without tail feathers? A cardinal without all that distinctive appendage?

Yes, it was true. Bobby had no tail feathers. How in the world, I wondered, could a cardinal fly without those all-important fins? But fly—and fight!—Bobby could, and did. Like a lot of us who are handicapped in one way or another, Bobby adjusted in a marvelous fashion. He became even more feisty than cardinals usually are. Bobby stood his ground. He chased away all who would challenge his turn at the table, even those aggressive jays.

I often wondered how Bobby lost his tail feathers. A scrap with a cat? Caught in somebody's cardinal-tail trap? I'd never know. As the weeks passed it became evident that Bobby was growing a new set of tail feathers. At first, they were barely visible. Then, slowly, they became more evident. Bobby was, in fact, growing a new tail! Glory be.

Bobby, of vocal and feisty witness to the wonders of nature.

And now meet Spunky. Spunky the Sparrow. Spunky the swallow-tailed sparrow. Spunky the super-swallow-tailed sparrow. And it grieves me to have to report that I suspect I now must say "the late" Spunky the Sparrow. For, you see, Spunky showed up missing just a couple of mornings ago, scarce a week since we'd been introduced. I say "showed up missing" because Spunky is still very much alive in memory.

I first noticed Spunky when he was muscled out of the crowd of sparrows who were scrapping to get to the head of the line at our feeder. Rather than fly off and return, Spunky fell to the ground, where he remained until all the others were gone. Then, with great effort, Spunky would fly, or attempt to, back to the feeder.

As the days passed, Spunky would try to fly but couldn't quite pull it off. He'd get airborne for a few feet and then collapse. He'd spin in circles and then, breathing hard, be forced to give it up. Only always, after brief rests, he'd try again and again and again.

For three days I placed food and water near Spunky, checking often to see if he was still among us. Finally, one morning this week, Spunky was nowhere to be found. I've not seen him since.

Spunky, of grand witness to the dignity that can be found in death.

Not a grackle is lamed.

Not a cardinal is injured.

Not a sparrow falls.

—*Arkansas Democrat-Gazette*, October 17, 1992.

CHAPTER X

Higher Ground

Too low they build, who build beneath the stars.
—Edward Young (1742)

1

Religion: What's It All About, Anyway?

This is probably going to shock you, so you might want to get ready: Sometimes I go through an entire day without thinking, even once, about the doctrine of original sin. Or predestination. Or who authored those obscure books in the Bible. Or whether the water really turned into wine. Or if the ax head actually floated. Or what Adam said when asked to surrender a rib.

In fact, I can recall whole half days in a row when such things as damnation, redemption, heaven, hell, existentialism, and the virgin birth were less than uppermost in my mind. I'm not particularly proud to make these confessions, especially in print. But I must also say that I'm not particularly ashamed to do so, either.

All this has to do with a topic that does, in fact, occupy more of my prized retirement time than I enjoy giving up—time I'd rather spend tinkering and piddling. That topic is expressed in tough questions, nagging questions that intrude upon my cherished time: What, after all, is this business of religion really all about? What does it really mean to be a Christian? Or a Jew. Or a Muslim. Or a member of whatever religion one might mention.

(Since the religious orientation of the great majority of Arkansans is Christianity, I'll confine these comments to that religion. However, I suspect that these thoughts are applicable to other faiths.)

As with a lot of knotty issues, perhaps it's easier to reverse the questions asked above—to ask what being a Christian *doesn't* mean. Herewith some opinions. Being Christian doesn't mean that one must be able to recite, chapter and verse, the scriptures, doctrines, creeds, and beliefs relating to the faith. Being Christian doesn't mean that one must be able to out argue and out debate those with different opinions on the fine points of doctrine.

Nor does "being a good Christian" necessarily have a lot to do with how much time one spends praying, reading the Bible, and doing good works—though such activities may indeed reflect one's commitment. Nor—dare I say it?—does being a good Christian hang on how much money one gives to the church.

What, then, *does* it mean to be a Christian?

Having confessed to not claiming a corner on answers to that question, I'll be bold enough to offer some ponderings on this most personal topic.

Being Christian has more to do with *being* than it does with *doing*, though doing is vital to expressing one's faith. Christianity's meaning is discovered by incarnating—by becoming—such realities as love, justice, mercy, forgiveness, reconciliation, service, sacrifice.

Is purity of deed and thought a test of the "good Christian?" Gosh I hope not. But I do believe that childlikeness is. And so is joy. And wonder. And openness. Openness to God, to self, and to others—perhaps most notably to those of other faiths or of no faith. And openness to life.

Now it's your turn: What, really, is *your* religious faith all about? Make notes. There'll be an exam.

—*Arkansas Gazette,* May 25, 1991.

2

Time for Some Jesus Stories

It's a family story, one of those oft-repeated tales that keep alive the memories of a distant past. (Oft-repeated to the extent that I've told this story before in this column, some years ago, as I recall.)

The time was the mid-1930s. The place was Magazine Mountain in Logan County, where our family has a cabin, the site of many happy times. The event was a close encounter of the scary kind. Precisely, a close encounter with a bobcat. Nay, a mountain lion. A real, live, angry, ferocious, horrendous mountain lion. A mountain lion as big as an elephant. The kind of mountain lion that eats little children. You know the kind.

It happened like this. A bunch of us—summer residents from big cities like Magazine, Conway, and Fort Smith—decided a night-time hike, a moonlight outing, would be fun. Into Bear Hollow. (The very name still makes the skin crawl.)

But not to worry. Our parents and several other big people were with us. No problem. We—my nine-year-old brother, two years my elder, and I—were brave, as were most of our little friends, except the girls. Courageous was the word. If need be, we could not only protect our younger brother, age two, but also our parents and our whole party of stalwart explorers.

That was before our dog treed the mountain lion. And before the night was rent by the most ferocious scream—in the tree just above our heads—ever heard by the ears of man, or of woman, either, for that matter. That was just before we two brave soldiers jumped seventeen feet straight into the arms of our parents. To protect them, of course.

Later that night, safe at last and being tucked into bed by our father, we made known our deepest need: "Daddy, would you please tell us some Jesus stories?"

It's like that, isn't it. When we are scared out of our wits, it's the Jesus stories—it's those familiar, ancient tales from our religious tradition—that give us the greatest comfort.

We're in such a time now. A lot of us, throughout this world, are scared out of our wits. We need to hear some Jesus stories. Some Moses stories. Some whoever stories from whatever religious tradition has brought strength, courage, hope, faith, and purpose to those who have gone before us.

Who, in this time of crisis, will tell us what we need most to hear? That chore, of course, is the duty of every member of the religious community. If that includes you, that means you. You are to be a teller of the stories of faith. And justice. And reconciliation. And love. And peace. You are to say to the community of faith: "Remember who you are."

It's strange, about these Jesus stories. And I suspect the same is true of the stories of other faiths. These stories comfort us in unusual and sometimes paradoxical ways. Sometimes the comfort is gentle, as in "Come unto me all ye who labor and are heavy laden and I will give you rest." But sometimes the comfort is harsh, making us listen again to see if this is really comfort we're being offered: "Love your enemies. Bless those who persecute you. Bless, and curse not."

Know any "Jesus stories"—or hope-giving, purpose-giving stories from whatever religious tradition you hold? Now is the time to tell them. Better still, now is the time to live them.

—*Arkansas Gazette,* February 2, 1991.

3

Religious Doubt: Foe or Friend?

There's the story about the old reprobate, the town atheist, who became desperately ill, took a turn for the worse, lingered near death for a time, and then suddenly pulled out of it. His wife's people, all upstanding church members, gathered around their in-law, long an embarrassment to the family. Citing the miraculous healing, the kinfolks announced that the old man most assuredly had been "saved by the Lord for a purpose."

"Yes, the Lord's got a work for you to do," the in-laws chimed in chorus. Nothing could have riled the old man more. "Well, he responded adamantly and with vigor, "I'll durn sure not do 'er!"

I've always liked that story, even though I side with "the Lord's got something for each of us to do" school. I find myself empathizing with the crusty old reprobate. It's one thing to accept willingly one's own assignments from the Lord. It's another thing altogether to have others, claiming to speak on the Lord's behalf, lay such assignments on us.

What is it that makes this old codger's strong-minded stubbornness so winsome and appealing? What's going on in this old man's obstinacy? It has to do, I suggest, with one of God's most significant—and at the same time most troublesome yet beautiful—gifts to us humans: The gift of doubt.

A recent note from a friend brought the topic to mind. Attached was a clipping from this newspaper, a Billy Graham column in which the veteran evangelist responded to a writer's questions about doubt. "I have lots of doubts," the writer confessed. "Sometimes I even wonder if any of it (the Christian religion) is true, or if it is just something people have made up."

Graham responded that although doubt can destroy faith, "it also can prod you to overcome your doubts and have greater faith." Later in the column was this statement by Graham, underlined by my friend: "Remember that the opposite of doubt is faith." My friend, in his handwritten note, suggested that the statement "needed a response" and added, "Since I leave all of my 'religious' thinking to you, I thought I'd pass this on." (This is what you get for having friends.)

Okay, let's take on religious doubt.

Let us praise honest doubt. Let us rejoice in God's wonderful, if disturbing, gift of doubt. We suggest that doubt, rather than being the enemy—"the opposite of faith"—is a necessary companion to faith, a prerequisite to authentic, wholesome, maturing faith. Do not fear your doubts. Make friends with your doubts. Consider that doubt may, in fact, be the Holy Spirit prodding you toward a more complete faith, toward more marvelous discoveries.

Receive your doubts as valued way stations on your pilgrimage to the holy city, stepping-stones to greater understanding and faith. Possess your doubts; do not let them possess you. Examine your doubts. Challenge them in your mind. Test them in your heart. See how they wear on your hands.

And do not be troubled if your doubts dog your steps along your journey, ever nipping your heels. Even doubts need to be loved.

—*Arkansas Gazette*, July 14, 1990.

4

Good News for Us Liars and Sinners

I see by the mail that my secret's out. I'm a liar. It was in this newspaper. A letter to the editor. A couple of weeks ago. I hope you missed it.

But, anyway, I guess I've been caught. Dead to rights, as they say. I'd been trying to keep it quiet, this lying weakness, but I guess that's just not to be. That's the way it goes with life—you tell a little lie and sooner or later the truth is out and the whole world knows about it. It even gets in the newspapers.

Only I've got another problem. It's not that I've let that letter bother me (haven't given it a second thought, as you can see), but I've spent some fairly uncomfortable nights trying to figure out just exactly which one of my lies has been discovered. If I knew which lie it was, I'd have a clue as to how to try to wiggle out of it. It's not a happy predicament, as perhaps you just might be able to understand.

Nor is it an enjoyable exercise, this trying to remember all the lies you've ever told during your entire life.

It could have been that one about the apple pie, though I'm at a loss to know how anybody but Mother ever knew about that. Or perhaps it was the one about the baseball and the window. The neighbors must have squealed; that's it. Or maybe it was those little fibs—I guess they were lies, actually; and yes, Your Honor, there were several—that had to do with homework. But that was a long time ago, if that counts.

Or, do you suppose it might even have been some of those solemn things I affirmed, right to the bishop himself and in front of all those people dressed in their Sunday best, when I enlisted as one of John Wesley's finest? Wesley lived back in the eighteenth century, you know, and had some pretty old-fashioned ideas, as you can see by these questions all Methodist preachers have since been asked:

"Are you going on to perfection?" I answered yes, like you're supposed to, and, judging by the record, that certainly could have been a lie. But at the time, I sort of believed it and still do. I just didn't realize it was going to be such a long trip.

"Are you in debt so as to embarrass you in your work?" I said no, like all the rest of my lying friends who were lined up there in front of their future employers. I guess that's it; the lie I've been found out in.

There have been other lies, of course. But if I were to tell you about them, I'd have to lie several times again, and, as we've just seen, that's not a pretty sight. Anyway, as long as I'm at it, let me tell you something else that's going to make you nervous: Not only am I a liar, I'm also a sinner. And if that's not enough to make your day, try this: I'm a liberal, too.

And what's more, hear this: I also happen to believe that Bill Clinton would make a pretty good president, for a Baptist, though I probably shouldn't mention such a thing in this present context. What politician needs to be endorsed by a lying, sinning, liberal preacher-columnist?

Anyway, dear friends, do have a nice day. I know I will. I'm already feeling better, having gotten my conscience clear. Mostly. At any rate, it's nice to remember that God has a pretty good record when it comes to dealing with us liars and sinners. I can only hope that Santa Clause is as forgiving.

—*Arkansas Democrat-Gazette*, December 14, 1991.

5

The Hunt for the Red-Hot Reverend

I see by the newspapers (this one, actually) that there's a hunt on for the best preacher—the best pulpiteer or sermonizer—in Arkansas. Well, it's about time. Actually, swarms of congregations have been engaged in that very endeavor for years, with unreported success.

If truth were known, Arkansas probably has about as many good preachers, give or take a passel, as are to be found. And the law of averages being what it is, it probably has as many of the other kind, too. Certainly the need is here. Fields white unto harvest, and all that.

But whatever, the search prompts some preaching. I happen to know that the folks at this newspaper are well aware that such a quest is fraught with pitfalls. Where angels fear to tread. Sermons, like good cooking and other works of art, aren't easily judged. "Best" is a slippery category when applied to matters more rightly judged in heaven. The way is straight and the gate is narrow.

Some stories come to mind. One has to do with the preacher

who, after a Sunday morning sermon, was greeted at the door by an enthusiastic member: "Oh, Brother Jones, every sermon you preach is better than the next one!" (Yes, I've told that one before, but a lot of you have bad memories.)

And then there was that fellow who said that although he'd never heard a sermon he didn't get something out of, he'd "sure had a lot of close calls." And, then again, there's the one about the congressman (a story that has nothing to do with preachers but for some reason comes to mind) who was publicly accused of being "the dumbest congressman in Washington." He protested: "I am not and I can prove it." Well, perhaps so. I suspect that determining who is the best preacher in Arkansas is sort of like determining who is the dumbest congressman in Washington.

But whatever one might think of sermon contests—and we're not sure what preachers like Amos, Ester, Jeremiah, Deborah, Jesus, and Paul might think—a secular society can benefit from such an enterprise. Two thoughts:

Thought One: It is refreshing to see a secular newspaper recognize the vital role that religion in general and preaching in particular plays in contemporary society. Good preaching helps society remember who it is and why it is. Good preaching helps society forge its values, define its goals, seek justice, and love mercy.

Preaching does, in fact, have a profoundly significant and important role in a secularized society. If a "best preacher" contest can further that realization, it will be a service rendered.

Thought Two: It is important that the public know what a truly demanding responsibility it is to be a preacher of good sermons (or a good preacher of sermons); what it is to comfort the afflicted while afflicting the comfortable; what it is to give encouragement, purpose, and hope and to be a bringer of good news.

God bless all preachers. May the "bad" ones improve; may the "good" ones get even gooder. But whatever, this word of caution to church members who nominate their pastor for the "best preacher" award: Beware—good preaching can be dangerous to one's health. Just remember what they did to that fellow from Galilee.

—*Arkansas Gazette*, March 31, 1990.

6

All Preachers Great and Small

It's been a whole week now and I think I'm going to get over it. I'm talking about the fact that I didn't win this newspaper's recent contest to discover the best preacher in Arkansas. Not only did I not win first place, I didn't even get second. Or third. Or any number, for that matter.

It's not that all this losing has bothered me, of course, or that I've even given it the least bit of thought. It's totally okay with me that I wasn't even mentioned. The fact that I didn't win, place, or show—or even get an honorable mention or win the Mr./Mrs. Congeniality Award—hasn't bothered me a bit. Not one little teeny-weeny bit. No siree. I've hardly even thought about the fact that I wasn't included. So don't worry about me. I'll be okay. Probably.

Anyway, my not winning may, in fact, be for the best. Now I'm in a position to empathize with, and perhaps even help, all you other losers out there. And that includes that multitude of soon-to-be-losers—those politicians who, after next week's primary elections, are going to be so down in the dumps over being dumped.

So it happens once again: The meek inherit the earth. The last come out first because of a hidden, secret prize.

In the best biblical tradition, all of us losers become winners—by becoming better equipped to help our fellow losers along the way. Don't get me wrong. It can be great to win. But—and this may come as a surprise—it also can be great to lose. How so, you ask? Herewith some thoughts on how losing needn't be all that bad:

Losing preserves the dream. Unlike winners, who swap their dream for an accomplishment, we losers still have our goal, our purpose, our golden shining dream. We get to keep trying. We get to keep dreaming. And that's not sour grapes. (At least I don't think it is.)

Losing can be more comfortable than winning. And that doesn't necessarily have to be a cop-out. Just think how tough it would be to have to get up in the pulpit every Sunday and realize, "These people have come to hear The Best Preacher (or second or third best) in Arkansas! Ohmygosh. What do I do now?" See—since I lost, that's just one more worry I don't have.

Losing helps us keep our perspective about ourselves. (We suspect the "best preacher" winners know this as well, and perhaps better, than the rest of us.) Losing reminds us that there's still work to do, that the task isn't yet accomplished.

The thought calls to mind the story about the preacher who, after delivering a rousing sermon in which he took great pride, said to his wife, "Honey, just how many truly great preachers do you think are alive today?" His wife responded: "I have no idea, but I know there's one less than you think there are." Losing can help all of us—and all us preachers great and small—keep our perspective.

Now if you'll excuse me, I've got to go practice up on my preaching. There just might be another "best preacher" contest any day now and I want to be ready.

—*Arkansas Gazette*, May 26, 1990.

7

Conversion and Murphy's Shoe Law

Now let's see if I've got this right. If I purchase this pair of comfortable walking shoes—this pair of eighty-dollar comfortable walking shoes—it would be smart of me to buy a second pair also. Because that way I'd get twice the wear from them. (This was me, talking with the shoe salesman.)

"That's right, sir, if you buy two pairs of these comfortable walking shoes you'll get double the wear." Oh, I see—I think. Buy two pairs, get twice the wear.

This was last week, and I'm not yet sure I've figured out exactly what the salesman meant. I think it had less to do with arithmetic than with Murphy's Shoe Law: One day of rest adds an extra day of life. Something like that.

I suppose I ought to believe this kind of logic because I've long practiced it: Work one day, take the next day off, and you can do twice the amount of work the following day. But whatever, this salesman didn't realize he was talking to a man who has to window shop for at least three months just to get in the mood to think seriously about buying even one pair of new shoes. A person to whom it has never, ever, occurred to buy two pairs of new shoes—especially eighty-dollar shoes—all at once. A person who remembers when seventeen dollars was the absolute most a Christian would pay for new shoes.

I guess the salesman's suggestion was really a compliment—like maybe he thought I was a Presbyterian or even an Episcopalian. Both of which groups, I've always imagined, buy at least two pairs of new shoes at every sitting.

But being from a long line of Methodists, I've never been able to interpret the verse, "How beautiful are the feet of those who bring good tidings," to mean that preachers were supposed to buy two pairs of new shoes at any one time. The very idea.

But whatever, again, I don't want to be unkind to the salesman. He was nice and I believe had my best interest at heart. But if I'd done as he suggested, I'd still be having sleepless nights. I'm hardly worthy of one pair of new shoes, to say nothing of two.

Actually, what we're talking about here is religion, in case you haven't already figured that out. And to stretch the connection even further, I cite another experience of this past week. The topic Sunday in the Sunday school class I attend was religious conversion—what it means to be "converted" or "born again." It was sort of a different topic for us, since most Methodists start squirming when such words are spoken out loud.

But anyway, the conversion topic is admittedly self-centered, in that it deals with the individual. That's where conversion occurs, isn't it—within an individual person? But just to be different, I expressed the opinion that this popular understanding of conversion is inadequate; that it's too person-centered, too individualized, too selfish, if you please.

My point: Religious conversation is a concept applicable not only to individuals but also to the larger realms of life. For instance, do not society's structures, its value systems, its institutions—including religious denominations—stand in need of conversion? Shouldn't the concept of conversion apply not only to individuals but also to such social blights as racism, greed, economic injustice, and ecological malpractice? Aren't such blights—such "evils"—proper candidates for conversion? Doesn't our nation need to be born again regarding such ills?

Can our appetites be converted? Can our "wants" be born again? I don't know—but we'd all better hope so.

So, what in the world does all this have to do with buying two pairs of shoes when one will do? Perhaps nothing. Perhaps everything.

But whatever, I like my new shoes. They're comfortable. I might even get over paying eighty dollars for them. But I hope I won't.

—*Arkansas Democrat-Gazette,* May 23, 1992.

CHAPTER XI

Other Journeys

When I was at home, I was in a better place;
but travelers must be content.
—William Shakespeare (1599)

1

On Planning Not to Sing in Tulsa

It was the headline above a small item in Monday's paper: "Singer has no plans to perform in Tulsa." About a vocalist who awoke one morning to read that he was to sing in Tulsa. No less than the lead role in "Fiddler on the Roof." The singer, who'd made no such plans, said the news left him "absolutely astounded, dumbfounded."

Well, I can imagine—and I can't even sing. Something about a contract having never been signed. That sort of thing. But whatever, the item prompted me to think about those not-too-few things that I have absolutely no plans whatsoever to do.

Yes, the number of my non-plans is innumerable. Those things that I have no plans to do. But if I were to make such a list, a list of things I have no plans to do, it would include the following, to cite only a few of my not-now-or-ever-to-be-planned activities.
I have no plans to:

> Become a candidate for bishop
> Jump off a bridge or anything else with a bungee cord tied around my
> 　　middle
> Enter the Mr. America contest
> Sing in public in Tulsa. Or elsewhere. Except, perhaps, from my back-
> 　　row pew in church, and then only when everyone else is singing real
> 　　loud

There are jillions of other things I have no plans to do, but perhaps the above is enough to prompt you to make your own list. And yes, you need to work on such a list. Things you have no plans to do.

The point of all this is to get you, and me, too, if I must, to ponder all those things that it would be well for us *to* do. Those things that we, in truth, *ought* to make plans to do. (Yes, this is the sort of thing you'd expect on the religion page. Someone trying to get you to do stuff you know you ought to do but aren't exactly excited about doing. But, look, this is my job. It's what I do. And it's not an especially tidy job, trying to get people like you to do the right thing, but somebody's got to do it.)

But enough. Today's agenda is serious: Things religious groups and individuals could make plans to do in response to the multitude of problems and issues symbolized by riots in Los Angeles and elsewhere.

An opinion: The remedies most relevant to such situations are those that religious groups may be expected to know best. Society has the right to look to religious institutions, and their members, to shed a special light on such darkness; to give analysis, insight, and wisdom; to offer guidance based on higher laws and larger values.

In short, to repeat a theme often sounded in this corner, now is the time for all religious groups to be, in the fullest sense, good pastors, good prophets, and good priests. And what does that mean? It means bringing comfort to those who suffer, hope to those who've lost hope, and encouragement to all. It means denouncing injustice. It means voicing the biblical indictment "Thou art the man"— whether the culprits are those responsible for entrenched economic, social, and political injustice and greed or those guilty of lawlessness in the streets.

Being pastors-prophets-priests means addressing long-neglected legitimate grievances. It means exposing and denouncing the sins of racism, classism, power-hoarding, and injustice of every stripe. It means calling the nation to prayer, to confession, to conversion, to reconciliation. It means sounding the ancient truth that righteousness exalts a nation and that sin is a reproach to its people. It means keeping faith alive.

Yes, it's okay to not make plans to do everything. It is terribly important, however, to make plans to do right things. And then to do them.

—*Arkansas Democrat-Gazette*, May 16, 1992.

2

On the Chance to Do It All Over Again

I've always thought that if I could do it all over again I'd do it pretty much the same way. Most of it, anyway. But I've changed my mind. I've now decided that if I could do it all over again I'd do it differently. At least a bunch of it.

You didn't ask, but here are a few of the things I'd do differently if given another chance.

I'd try to be a nicer, sweeter, better person. (I threw that in right at the top to please my relatives.) I'd try to do more good deeds, help more people, be more loving, not be so self-centered, etc. And I'd try not to feel self-righteous about how good I was.

Then, after I'd gotten all that sweetness out of my system, I'd have more fun. I'd play more, laugh more, and probably cut up more—and, yes, probably embarrass myself more, if that's possible. And I'd not feel guilty about it.

I'd try to be more generous. Not so possessive. I'd be a kinder, gentler person, even if it meant asking help from the Republicans. And I wouldn't be apologetic for being such a dandy fellow.

I'd be both easier and more difficult to get along with, depending on what love might require. For example, if love required that I be a more easy-going person, I'd try to be that. But if love required that I be more stubborn, more adamant about my convictions, more hardheaded—even though it upset a lot of people—I'd try to be that way.

Specifically, if I could do it all over again, I'd be more outspoken against injustice. I'd be more outraged at how society cheapens life. I'd be more indignant about the terrible damage we've done to this lovely planet. If I could do it all over again, I'd try harder to be God's Really Angry Man at all those things God wants us to be really angry about. And I'd try to be God's Really Sweet Person regarding those things we're meant to be really sweet about. And I'd let the chips fall where they might.

If I could do it all over again, I'd read more books, old and new. I'd become better acquainted with the Bible and its ancient yet living wisdom. And I'd seek truth in the company of modern-day pilgrims and sojourners, of whatever stripe.

I'd observe more silent times. I'd spend more nights in my mountain tree house, lying on my back watching the stars. I'd smell more flowers, climb more mountains, soar higher and farther in my sailplane, hike more trails, sail my thirty-six-foot ketch to never-discovered islands in the South Pacific, ride my bicycle the length of the Great Wall of China and perhaps surf the north shore of that Hawaiian island where the really big waves come crashing in.

I'd do my churchgoing differently. I'd be more aware of what the presence of others has to say. I'd be both more and less critical of the sermon, more loving toward the preacher.

But, of course, it doesn't work this way. There's no way any of us is going to be allowed to do it all over again. There are, however, some things each of us can do about the remaining time given to us. We can fill these days and nights with deeper, more significant, more lasting meanings. We can reinvigorate them with high purpose. And with joy. We can infuse them with redemption, nobleness, and love.

All together now, let us sing: "This little light of mine, I'm gonna let it shine, let it shine, let it shine, let it shine."

—*Arkansas Gazette*, July 21, 1990.

3

When the Storms of Life Are Raging

I would have gotten to this chore earlier, but I've been outside picking up limbs and branches. From last night's windstorm. That storm that messed up my lovely yard, my yard I'd cleaned so nicely just a couple of days ago. That storm that left leaves and junk all over my pretty patio. My pretty patio I'd swept clean only last evening.

Oh my, oh my, the troubles I've seen.

So if this column is late, don't blame me. Blame You Know Who. Blame the One responsible for those pesky winds that wreaked havoc with my playhouse. Blame Whoever it was that had the impertinence to pay no attention whatsoever to my carefully laid plans for the day. Plans that didn't allow time—not one moment, much less a whole hour!—for cleaning up after Somebody's thoughtless summer storms.

No wonder this country's in such a mess. No wonder the Republicans can't get their act together. So much for the best-laid plans.

But perhaps my grievous woes may be used to examine a larger issue: What, indeed, does one do when life's plans—life's really important plans—are interrupted? What does one do when good things are planned, happy times anticipated, and life takes a different turn? What does one do when the dreaded "I didn't count on that" syndrome suddenly occurs?

Let me illustrate the issue by shifting from the trivial windstorm event noted above to a truly serious instance of how life's plans can be so suddenly interrupted. The other evening, shortly before midnight, our telephone rang, waking me from sleep. A relative in Tennessee was on the line: "Cousin John, you're the closest contact I have with The Man Upstairs and I need a miracle."

I wanted to interrupt and quip to my cousin that if I was his closest such contact, he was in bad shape, indeed, but I didn't. I sensed he had serious news.

He did. With grief in his voice, my cousin told of how his business partner's youngest child, a five-year-old daughter, was at that moment clinging to life after a tragic accident earlier that day. "I need a miracle," my cousin said, choking the tears. Would I pray for this child and for her parents?

I'm sure that when that particular morning began, those parents and their friend, my cousin, didn't schedule time for the events that were to transpire on that sad day. A telephone call the next afternoon brought the news that the child had died.

Life interrupted. Whole lives changed, never to be the same again. Plans altered in an ultimate way. And what of the miracle my cousin had sought? What's to be said now?

Perhaps there is no way, nor should there be, that mere words can assuage the grief experienced at such a time. But we at least can ponder the question: What of miracles sought and "not granted"?

Upon reflection I would say this to my cousin: No, the miracle did not come as you wanted, but ponder this. Another miracle was working, and continues to work. It is the miracle of love—the miracle that enabled you to stand by your friends; the miracle that made you cry; the miracle that prompted your telephone call; the miracle of parents' love that is so strong that even death cannot destroy it.

Only love can bring us such pain. Only love can make us hurt so deeply. Only love can cause us such grief.

Some things can wait—such as cleaning yards, sweeping patios, and writing newspaper columns. Other things, however, shouldn't be put off. Things like supporting each other in our common times of need. Like telling loved ones and friends how much they mean to us. How much we love them.

—*Arkansas Democrat-Gazette*, August 15, 1992.

4

Again Last Week

Okay, already, I know it. I've pushed this retirement theme to the limit. So what if you're retired, Workman, what's the big deal? People retire every day.

I don't. This is my first. So you've got a decision to make: You can either read a bit more about all this or you can turn to the comics. It's a free country.

It happened again last week. I should have been ready but wasn't. A friend died. Unexpectedly. A car accident in a distant state.

This newspaper's reception to mark my retirement and welcome my successor was a fine occasion, attended by friends from the religious community and colleagues at the paper. Everybody behaved themselves admirably. Some important people said some nice things about James Scudder, my successor, and about me. And good food and fellowship abounded.

Afterward, Liz and I decided that, what the heck, we'd top off the evening with yet one more wild and crazy celebration. We'd eat out. We drove home to Conway and, for the first time since our college days forty years ago, dined at Stoby's. Stoby's famous neighborhood sandwich and eat shop.

Liz said she'd like to have a taco salad, small, and a glass of iced tea, please. I said what the heck again, this is a celebration, so I'll have the same. Afterward, we drove the five blocks home, loafed a bit, and then took a ride on our bicycles. As often on these evening rides, we found ourselves on the lovely campus of Hendrix College, our alma mater, so rich with memories.

Virginia, you really were something else, something special. Though you'd be the last to admit it, you were one of those people who enrich life for others simply by the quiet, dignified, meaningful manner in which you lived. What a blessing, your life. What a shock, your death.

Yet how meaningful that here on this campus, where so long you worked and where your professor husband taught for so many years—how meaningful that here, on last Saturday, your family and friends should gather to celebrate your life and draw strength from the ages.

During Monday evening's lazy bicycle ride I thought of Virginia and Jimmy Upton and remembered A. E. Houseman's lines, which first I heard nearly a half century ago on this campus:

> With rue my heart is laden for golden friends I had. For
> many a rose-lipt maiden and many a lightfoot lad.
> By brooks too broad for leaping the lightfoot boys are laid;
> the rose-lipt girls are sleeping in fields where roses fade.

Yes, Virginia. Yes, Jimmy. You and the other rose-lipt maidens and lightfoot lads enriched our lives beyond measure. You did well your work. Rest in peace.

And you'll know, won't you, that our slow-motion cycling through your gardens, peopled by so many memories, are part of our celebration of all that you were. And of all that you, and that great company of others who touch life with beauty, continue to be.

—*Arkansas Gazette,* August 5, 1989.

5

Nobody Lives Forever—Even Mothers

The call came at 11:40 P.M., waking me from deep sleep. "Mr. Workman, there's been a change in your mother's condition. You need to come to the hospital right away." No, they couldn't be more specific. "The doctor will talk with you when you get here."

The surgery, two days earlier, had gone well. Mother, just five days from her ninety-first birthday, was recovering. Alert most of the time. Good spirits. No pain, she said, though I wondered if that were really the truth.

But now, arriving at the hospital just before midnight, I thought, "Oh, no. I'm really not ready for this." All was going so well. A young hospital attendant—he later told me he was a third-year college student and hoped to go to medical school—met me as the elevator doors opened.

"Mr. Workman? If you'll come with me, please, to the nurses' station." I didn't ask. I didn't want him to have to tell me.

Another young person, a nurse, was next. "Mr. Workman, let's go to the waiting room down the hall, please." It was time to ask. "What's the situation? What's happening?" Thankfully, she leveled with me. Gently. Stopping right there in the corridor, she told me. A heart stoppage. They worked with her for twenty minutes. Couldn't revive her. The doctor would tell me more.

Mother was dead. I'd feared it, I suppose, when the telephone first rang.

Shock. You knew this would come; it had to, someday. Nobody lives forever. Even mothers. And besides, John, you're almost sixty-four. You're supposed to be a big boy by now, aren't you?

Mother was still in her room, they said, and, yes, I could go in. We had visited there only brief hours earlier. It'd been a good visit, with neighbors calling by. Now, Mother still lay in her bed, her arm still warm to my touch.

A few moments of silence. Then, a brief word—Have a pleasant journey, Mother—and a kiss on the forehead.

A phone call home. Conversation with the doctor, each of us, I believe, trying to comfort the other. The doctor's words were helpful; the tears in his eyes were more so.

It was okay, Mother. It's all right to die. We'd talked about such things. We both knew it was okay.

A long life well lived. So little suffering. So much time to enjoy wonderful memories—husband, friends, her own family, children, grandchildren, great-grandchildren, her beloved home. No regrets. Tears, yes, but tears of joy as well as loss.

"You'll have to excuse me," I told the nurse and attendants as I choked up signing the papers. "I don't do this every day." They understood, they said, and I believed them. It helped.

The following few days were a time of genuine celebration—so many friends, so many kind expressions, so many memories recalled. On the evening before the funeral, children, grandchildren, great-grandchildren, and other family members joined in a joyous "things remembered" session.

At the graveside the birds sang marvelously. I'd swear those cardinals flew from Conway to Little Rock just to sing the same wonderful songs Mother enjoyed each morning on the patio at home.

I suppose it's selfish to impose such personal experiences on others. In the past, as I've heard others give such details of a loved one's passing, I could never quite understand why they did it. Now I know. It's part of the necessary ritual. Something that has to be done.

You didn't ask to hear all this; but I needed to tell it.

—*Arkansas Gazette,* June 22, 1991.

6

Of Magic Rocks and Other Things Lost

Among other things, I'll remember 1990 as the year I lost my magic rock. Only I didn't really lose it—though I did, in a way. In fact, 1990 may have been the year I truly found my magic rock.

Although I haven't yet located this treasure, which I misplaced sometime during the spring of the late year, I've discovered another marvelous wonder: You really can't lose a magic rock. And magic is, in fact, what my prized rock most surely was. Or is.

I suppose that having written the above, I'll have to confess regarding this magic rock business. This means I'll probably lose whatever might remain of my reputation as a sort of religious person, orthodoxly speaking.

Oh, well.

You see, I've believed in magic rocks since I was old enough to pick up stuff. Rocks, mainly. Since baby days I've been a rock picker-upper. Mostly I pick up just the magic ones, though the others also have their appeal.

Time would fail me to tell of the myriad rocks, magic and ordinary, that decorate my study. I'll limit myself to the prize stone cited above. This magic rock was—is—rather small, about the size of a young pecan, though not as symmetrical. It is light in color, almost white. And, behold, this rock possesses the most magical of all qualities: It glistens with hundreds, perhaps thousands, of little "points of light," as George would call them.

When held at the proper angle to any light—the sun, a lamp, a candle—my magic rock bursts into joyous life, its multitudes of tiny windows shining brightly. Surely little switches are clicked on and tiny beings open their curtains to let me know they are home, snug and warm.

My rock even came with batteries included. It glistens in the dark, in its own magical way.

I don't recall how I came upon this particular magic rock. I do know, however, that it came into my life at a time of need. A dark time. It came some four years ago, soon after I learned I had cancer. It was there throughout that ordeal. It was in my pocket as I traveled hundreds of miles to a hospital. It was there at my bedside, through long dark nights and during interminable weeks when I thought that all earthly lights might, in grim fact, be turned off.

There it was, my magic rock, to remind me of the many, many lights that had blessed, and continued to bless, my life. The light of love. Family. Faith. Friends. The light of wonder. Mystery. Adventure. The light of work. Of play. The lamps of learning. Remembering. Forgetting.

Some would caution me that it's silly, at best, to speak of a magic rock. That the magic is not in the rock but in the reminding, the calling to consciousness, the remembering. They are right, of course. Aren't they? (I know, however, that my rock does in fact have magical powers. What else, other than magic, could cause me to clean out my desk, my closet, my car, my workshop, and my storeroom in a months-long effort to find such a humble prize?)

Somewhere out there my magic rock is still doing its work. Sort of like the lamp in the Temple. And the star of Bethlehem.

—*Arkansas Gazette*, January 5, 1991.

7

Leavin' on a Jet Plane

Get ready, I've got some news. This is my last column. That's right. It's like the country music song says: "If your phone don't ring, it's me." Only in this case, if you don't read any more "Chasing Fireflies" columns in this corner, I'm the fellow who won't be writing them. No more "Chasing Fireflies." I'm hanging it up.

Now, silly you, stop that sobbing. It's not all that bad. It's not exactly the end of the world. (If, however, uncontrollable grief is not your major reaction to this news—if it's more like "Whoopee!"— then this word to you: It serves you right, you old so-and-so.)

Just kidding, in that last sentence. But I'm not kidding about quitting. I'll try to get serious and explain, at least in part.

After twenty years as a pastor and another nineteen years and two weeks as a journalist—six years as editor of the *Arkansas Methodist* newspaper, ten years as religion editor at the *Arkansas Gazette* (and two additional years as a weekly columnist there), and one year and two weeks as a religion columnist in this newspaper— I've decided to quit chasing fireflies in print and do it full time in reality.

Fireflies were meant to be chased outdoors, not inside on a computer.

Some quick arithmetic: During my almost twenty years in newspapering I've written somewhere in the neighborhood of 1,300 columns (two each week while at the *Methodist*), hundreds of feature stories, multitudes of interviews, and oodles of news articles and other pieces. By most measures, that's plenty. By some, it's way too many.

For someone who couldn't wait to get out of school so he wouldn't have to write term papers, it boils down to this, mostly: I'm weary of deadlines. I'm tired of pushing this boulder up the hill every week. It's time to jump out of the way before it squashes me.

It's not been easy, this decision to quit. But recently it came to me out of the blue: John, you're spending way too much time debating the matter. It's time. Just go ahead and give it up.

Regrets? Certainly. Already have them. Already miss it—and I haven't even finished this column. But I've a remedy for that. Come every Tuesday morning, I'll probably sit myself down in front of this keyboard and keep on writing columns. As a dandy ditty puts it, "The sweetest songs I've ever sung are still inside my head." But now I won't have to meet deadlines.

But the question persists: Why in the world would anyone give up such a great forum as a weekly newspaper column? What a privilege! What an opportunity! No arguments there. Anyone who'd give up such an honor would have to be a fool.

Shake hands with a fool.

A wise person said it: Every ending is a prelude to a new beginning. I'm already getting excited about my next new beginning. Maybe work on a book. Write one, that is. Might even read one, too. Maybe do some freelance writing. And I'll putter. But I was already doing bunches of that. So what—I'll putter some more.

And maybe now, at long last, I'll finally be able to go full time on the rodeo circuit. Who knows. Or, since I understand that in some societies the elderly are venerated, perhaps I'll just hang around and wait to be venerated.

Any parting wisdom? Yes: Don't give up on religion. On the church, synagogue, masjid, or other. And don't even give up on newspapers. God, being God and in the redemption business, is still on the job.

A last word. It's something I've always wanted to put in print but never had the guts. This you don't want to miss. Here goes:

. . . Whoops. Hang on a second—there goes a late-season firefly past my window. If I hurry I bet I can catch it! Back in a moment. . . .

—*Arkansas Democrat-Gazette,* November 14, 1992.

CHAPTER XII

Up, Up, and Away
Through the Valley of the Sun

How much a dunce that has been sent to roam
excels a dunce that has been kept at home!
—William Cowper (1782)

A Good Breakfast Is Worth the Gamble

Where, if not in a casino, is a body supposed to get breakfast in Jackpot, Nevada? Where, in this Idaho-border last-chance gambling town (or first-chance, depending on whether you're traveling north or south), can a moral man dine without being surrounded by all that glitter and temptation that goes with ill-gotten gain? Where in Jackpot is one to eat if not in a casino? Nowhere—that's where.

So, trying my best (without success) to put my Wesleyan upbringing totally out of mind, I resigned myself to necessity, hunger at this point being stronger than morality. After passing at least four casinos, I idled Frontier Scout, my faithful motorcycle, into the parking lot of the last betting establishment on the southern edge of this small outpost town. I glanced guiltily over my right shoulder, then over my left, didn't see Clint Eastwood or anybody else from my Sunday school class, so I hitched up my jeans and snuck myself right inside that real-life casino. Right through those double-swinging doors I went. God knows I'm sorry.

To make sense out of this tale, I've got to stop here and back up a bit. Back to the beginning. No, not back to Adam and Eve, but at least back a couple of weeks before this Second Fall of Man. I've got to back up and tell you what this is all about.

What all this is about is a motorcycle trip. A dandy motorcycle trip. A grand adventure—even if I did have to actually go inside a casino to get breakfast.

The year was 1996. Departure date for our two-brothers blast-off from Conway, Arkansas, was June 24 at 7:20 A.M. Not bad—only fifty minutes late for the scheduled 6:30 A.M. exit. My younger brother, Wally, then age sixty-three, a retired lawyer out of Houston,

.

Author's note: The essays in this chapter, written after my "full" retirement, have not been previously published, with the exception as noted at the end of this first essay.

Texas, and myself, then sixty-eight. Headed for Idaho we were! Off to visit our older brother Jim.

Wally, mounted on his spiffy candy-apple red Honda Gold Wing, his six cylinder, 1500 cc supercycle. Me on my dinky fourteen-year-old two-cylinder, 450 cc, dull-gray Suzuki (self-modified with all sorts of homemade gadgets and loaded like one of those Dust Bowl–era vehicles headed for the Good Life.)

(Guess which brother went to law school and which to seminary.)

What a great trip it was! A marvelous adventure. You'll have to wait to read more about it. By the time I returned fourteen days later (Wally remained in the northwest; his wife flew up from Houston to join him for some touring in Canada), I'd traveled almost 5,000 miles. Almost all of those miles being on those marvelous little-traveled "blue" highways. Only about 250 miles on busy interstate freeways.

But we were talking about breakfast. A casino breakfast.

I'd left Twin Falls, Idaho, about an hour and a half earlier that morning at first light, having had only a half cup of cold Tang and a mashed-up granola bar (emergency food probably not more than a couple of years old). This to tide me over till I got down the road a bit. Down to where, in gambling country, a man could get a proper breakfast. The kind of breakfast real cowboys eat every day.

(Actually, the eggs and sausage and coffee and toast and jelly and jam and sweet roll and second cup of coffee and another sweet roll were really great. Even tasted better than that sissy food you get in those moral restaurants. And they almost gave it to me— doubtless figured me, the moment I sauntered in, as one of those early-morning big spenders.)

This was a special day for me. July 4, 1996. My sixty-ninth birthday. (This reflection is being written about four years later; I'm now seventy-three). Born on the Fourth of July, I was. A Yankee Doodle Dandy. Such a day merits a special breakfast.

Early in the planning of this trip, when it was still little more than a dream, I'd spent hours studying maps, seeking the most inviting, the most enticing routes. Routes I'd never traveled before. I'd learned long ago that such planning and anticipation can be one of the most enjoyable aspects of any adventure.

For my solo route home, I kept considering what seemed (to me, anyway) a remote highway down the eastern edge of Nevada. New country to me. Unknown. Mysterious. Was it desert? High plateaus? Were gas, food, and water available on the long stretches between those small settlements, those tiny dots on the map? I didn't know the answers to any of those questions, and I'm sure that's what made the route so appealing. The lure, the challenge, the excitement, the risk of the unknown. Yea, though I cycle through the valley of the sun. . . .

I spent my sixty-ninth birthday on that route, and it will be a birthday I will cherish until memory fails. For hour after hour I floated through a dreamlike world of unsurpassably beautiful scenery. On and on I rode, sometimes as far as fifty miles or more without seeing another vehicle or human being. I sailed silently (it seemed), almost in a trance, through vast valleys—some I guessed to be a dozen miles wide—bounded on both sides by high, snow-capped mountains.

Far in the distance I watched weather systems form in the July heat. I rode hypnotized by lightning and rain showers that cavorted about until they finally played themselves out. I weaved through magnificent rock formations, through desert wastes, and occasional lush meadows. Often I would see elk, antelope, or deer—a not infrequent sight during our travels throughout the several western states.

My sixty-ninth birthday ended in central Utah. I had enjoyed a four-hundred-mile banquet of beauty laid out for my solitary feasting. The passage was blest by frequent thoughts of family—my wife, our four children, and five grandchildren (with number six due soon)—and by recalling so many good times with loved ones and friends. Showers of blessings indeed.

So, you see—all this in testimony to the benefits of a good breakfast. Mother always told me that breakfast was the most important meal of the day. This one was a gamble that sure paid off.

(Portions of this essay appeared in the *Log Cabin Democrat*, December 8, 1996.)

—Conway, Spring 2000

2

On the High Seas with *The Ode to Joy!*

A brisk wind aft, the lee rail under. The following seas lift the stern; the taught vessel surfs down the ever-building wave, finally slips off the crest, and balks in that momentary lull before starting the process all over again with the next wave. Racing with the spray, she was. A bone in her teeth, as the old salts say.

On the high seas with *The Ode to Joy!* Thrill upon thrill.

Perhaps I should tell you that *The Ode to Joy!*, a sailing vessel, is all of seven feet, nine inches long. And the high seas upon which she is sailing, in the breathtaking account above, is Beaverfork Lake near Conway, Arkansas. Beaverfork Lake, perhaps a mile and a half long and about six hundred yards across at the widest, might fall a wee bit short of being high seas. But landlocked though it be, when the wind is up and the seas are rolling, Beaverfork could be the South Atlantic, the perilous waters off the Horn. Rounding the Horn on Beaverfork Lake, I was.

And *The Ode to Joy!* Aye, matey, she is pure poetry, she is. Pure poetry in motion. Liquid motion. Poetry in motion when on a broad reach, racing with the wind. Poetry in bone-jarring motion when strapped down, beating to windward for all she's worth, tossing spray high and wide, her skipper grim at the helm, face set against the fury of the elements, brushing salt spray from his hair. (Well, no salt spray, actually. And, well, no hair, either. But what the heck, this is poetry, not prose.)

Perhaps the reason I'm so in love with *The Ode to Joy!* is that I built her myself. About five years ago, way back in 1995 it was. Got the plans out of a book. A book by Harold "Dynamite" Payson, titled "Build the New Instant Boats." Dynamite told me, in the chapter titled "Nymph: A 7-Foot 9-Inch Mind Boggler," that he built the little craft in twenty-four hours and that I could do the same. Well, Dynamite didn't know me. It took me, by count, most of six weeks to do the job.

But what a joy the job was! It was about the third week, when the little craft's lines began to take shape and really show her off, that the name came to me out of the blue. "This boat *has* to be named *The Ode to Joy!*" It had been such a joy to fashion her, to mold her, to see her lines emerge in a symphony of beauty. This had to be *The Ode to Joy!* Beethoven would understand.

I must pause here to thank Jan, our church choir director, for providing me a tape recording of Beethoven's Ninth Symphony to be used on launch day, with, of course, all the attending appropriate ceremony. An excerpt of that really marvelous portion of the Ninth, approaching the conclusion, when the heavens open and that miracle of music pours forth to thrill the soul. Music worthy of being named after my little vessel. Beethoven would be so grateful, so indebted to me for immortalizing his creation, his genius. You're welcome, Ludwig.

Naturally, I had to improve on Dynamite's plan. I added a bowsprit, making a true sloop out of the little catboat design. For a mast I used a large bamboo pole salvaged from a city street right-of-way over near the campus of the University of Central Arkansas. Perfect for the *Ode.* A companion bit of bamboo made a proper boom. And a dandy crooked length of smaller bamboo was just right for the tiller. Sort of a South Pacific motif.

What to use for sails? I pondered. I posed the question to my paint dealer, who immediately came up with a solution. "I've got a tarp over here, been around for years, that I'll give you." Since I couldn't improve on the price, I took it gladly.

Bright blue, the tarp was, and is. After sizing and cutting, it made a perfect mainsail. Even enough left over for the little jib. Now, with the *Ode's* bright green hull, dark blue underbody, gray interior (decorated with splashes of varied colors), and shiny blue sails, the little vessel is a delight to the eye. At least to my eye. To both of my eyes, in fact.

When not on long voyages to the South Seas or across the Atlantic or cruising lazily among the Caribbean islands or across and back the blue Mediterranean or roughing it off the coast of Alaska, the *Ode* rests on our patio. Under a tarp purchased brand-new for the purpose. It looks like it's supposed to be there. Waiting. Waiting for the next good sailing day. Waiting for her skipper to quit all that fooling around in his study with unimportant stuff and come on out for a sail.

I'm ready, *Ode*. I'm rarin'. Let's do it.

—Conway, Summer 2000.

3

Travels with Bill

Over the past half dozen and more years of wanderings, both mental and otherwise, I've frequently had an unexpected fellow traveler along the way. An unexpected and uninvited, though not totally unwelcome, fellow traveler. And who might this mystery man be? Who other than Bill Clinton. President of the United States William Jefferson Clinton.

Bill—he calls me John during our travels—has shown up as I bicycled the Ozarks; as I motorcycled the American West; as I sailed the high seas of Faulkner County's Beaverfork Lake. And as Liz and I strolled through Conway's Laurel Park on our cherished evening outings, talking of this and that, here would come Bill again. Interrupting yet one more time. Grabbing my mind again. That's not nice, Bill. I was talking with Liz.

But Bill has a way of hanging about. He just won't leave me be. He keeps nudging in, messing up my thoughts, disturbing my mind, distracting and sometimes nearly ruining my travels. My travels, which are supposed to be fun and relaxing.

Bill, I thought we'd settled all this. When are you going to leave me be? Don't you realize I'm retired? This is one reason I quit writing in the newspapers—so I wouldn't have to deal with such stuff. Buzz off, Bill. Get a life. I've got important retirement things to do. Got to work on my motorcycle. Sail my boat. Tinker my bicycle. Work on my Magazine Mountain cabin. Clean up my shop.

And what do we talk about, Bill and I, when we travel together? Oh, my, oh, my, the list is so long. We talk about opportunities. Missed and taken. We talk about great accomplishments. We talk about disappointments. And anger and disbelief and outrage and embarrassment and frustration and anger again. And about other things.

As an Arkansan, and as one who once thought Bill Clinton would make a great leader, I try to tell Bill about my disappointment. And my anger. And then Bill, being Bill, says something that sounds like "same to you, Johnny boy." I shoot back that we're talking about him, not about me (even though I *was* talking about my anger).

Anyway, after the dust has mostly settled—after the months and even years have passed—I find that I've been overtaken by yet another Traveler. One who had been with us, Bill and me, all the way. But to date, anyway, this Traveler hadn't voiced his/her opinion on these matters. At least to the point that it got my attention. Not, anyway, until lately.

And that opinion? This Traveler had the gall to say something like "Let him who is without sin cast the first stone." Cheap shot, that one. And again: "Forgive seven times seventy." That sort of thing. Whole bunches of low blows and cheap shots. And so, one day I shoot back at Traveler: But we're talking about Bill Clinton here! Isn't this different?

Traveler, sighing, responds: Yes, it is. And no, it isn't. It's different, Traveler said, in that to whom much is given, much is expected. But it's not different, Traveler continued, in that there are no conditions, no exemptions regarding forgiveness. You either offer forgiveness or you don't. And if you don't, you're the one who's got the problem. Tough dude, this Traveler.

But I shot back again at Traveler: But what about my anger? Aren't I justified in being angry with Bill for having, in my assessment, messed up such a grand opportunity, what could have been such a wonderful record of achievements? And what about my anger at how Bill's sexual indiscretions—and his evasions and distortions of truth—have affected the children and youth of our country? And what about my anger at Bill's messing up the name of Arkansas and us Arkansans? Isn't my anger righteous anger? Isn't my indignation righteous indignation and therefore justified?

You know what Traveler said to all that? He said, No, it's not justified. He said, Sure, John, you're hurt. But what about those things

I said in that book I wrote? All those things about forgiveness and about redemption. You mean, John (Traveler still talking), that all those things don't apply to Bill? Or to you?

(Sometimes I don't know who's the most unwelcome and disturbing companion on a trip—Bill or Traveler.)

So, what's my bottom line now, Bill? I suppose it's something like this: You've got a whole lot of life left over after you complete your term as president. My hope for you now is much the same as it was back on July 11, 1992, when I wrote you a rather public private letter (when it appeared you'd be the Democrat's nominee for president). Here's part of what I said then and would repeat now, even though it sounds a bit preachy:

> Bill, I've long believed that one day you could make our nation a good president. Perhaps even a great one. But more important is that you be a good man. A good husband. A good father. I will be among the many who will be praying for you, and for our country, in these most important days. God bless you.

But whatever, Bill, I've changed my mind: Let's keep traveling together. There is still lots to talk about. We're both making progress. Maybe we can travel all the way to where the warm sunshine of redemption and renewal will finally light our way home.

—Conway, Spring 2000.

4

The Great Arkansas River Valley Explosion of '94

It happened almost seven years ago. The great Arkansas River Valley Explosion of '94. You probably heard about it. Maybe you even heard it. But if not, you need to know about it. Just for history's sake.

All this has to do with a project a friend and I have enjoyed for a number of years: Build a boat to float down the Arkansas River, maybe even on down the Mississippi to New Orleans! Huck Finn style. Dream of a lifetime.

So, when my friend purchased an old twenty-four-foot used party barge, we began a rebuilding project to prepare, in earnest, for the great voyage. The Great Voyage second in importance only to that of Hernando de Soto.

The two of us, both retired clergy, had kidded and joked with friends about the plan. On our voyage down the river we'd have revival meetings by day and casino gambling by night. Offer theology seminars and such. Lots of fun, kidding around. We'd sell tickets. Have a Celebrity of the Day event. Give cut-rate fees for weddings and baptisms. Lots of fun talk like that.

The kidding kept on. Everywhere we went around town friends would ask, "Been on the Great River Trip yet? No? Well, when?"

We even took a boating safety course, sponsored by the U.S. Coast Guard Auxiliary. We were serious. Still are. Keep the dream alive. But, anyway, back to the explosion.

What follows is a bogus news release (prepared for friends and family) about what was an actual, factual event in the course of our preparations for our grand adventure. Herewith that bogus news story:

NEWS FLASH—FOR IMMEDIATE RELEASE
MORRILTON, ARK., Oct. 3, 1994—What could have been a maritime disaster of major proportions was narrowly averted here today by the heroic action of two stalwart Arkansas seamen. The pleasure craft *The Nonesuch*, en route up the Arkansas River from Toad Suck Lock and Dam to Petit Jean Mountain, survived what the two crew members, both well-known and highly respected retired clergymen of Conway, termed "one hell of an explosion" while locking through Arkansas River Lock and Dam No. 9 at Morrilton.

The explosion came just as the two seamen, both cum-laude graduates of the U.S. Coast Guard Auxiliary Boating Skills and Seamanship Course (Class of 1994), started *The Nonesuch*'s motor to begin their exit from the lock. The explosion, at 4:37 P.M., was heard throughout the three-county Arkansas River Valley region.

Mr. Jon D. Guthrie, *The Nonesuch* owner and commander,

told reporters, who massed at the scene in immediate response to the earth-shattering noise, that his first reaction was to turn to crew chief Mr. John S. Workman and inquire calmly, "What the (heck) was that?" Mr. Workman, appearing calm and collected, though his face was streaked with soot and chemical fire retardant, told reporters that his first reaction was to offer an appropriate prayer and respond to Mr. Guthrie, "What was what?"

Mr. Guthrie said his next word was to say to Mr. Workman, "John, we're on fire!" Which, in fact, *The Nonesuch's* engine was.

Both seamen said they thought that another vessel that was also in the lock, a U.S. Corp of Engineers tugboat, had exploded. "We thought that whole dang tugboat had blowed itself up," the two said.

Federal authorities praised Guthrie and Workman for their quick action in putting out the fire. That action, which officials termed "of no small heroism," was accomplished within forty-five seconds after the explosion.

Preliminary reports indicate a gasoline leak, possibly at a fuel filter, caused the explosion. Although *The Nonesuch* had a backup motor, technical difficulties prevented the Conway seamen from using it, and the vessel exited the lock under oar power.

"That's the first time we've ever seen that," said the lockmaster as Mr. Workman rowed the eleven-foot "sweeps," successfully moving the twenty-four-foot vessel safely through the lock. "That's the way Christopher Columbus did it," shouted another lock attendant as the valiant seamen moved through the cavernous concrete chamber.

Guthrie and Workman reported that the event occurred on their initial experience in "locking through" the Arkansas River Navigation System. "They told us [at the Coast Guard Auxiliary school] it's be an unforgettable experience," the heroic seamen said.

End of news release. But not the end of the dream, which, though put on hold, is still alive. That's the nice thing about dreams. They pay benefits even before maturing. Often during those early days when we were restoring the barge, getting it ready for the mighty waters, we remarked, "You know, even if *The Nonesuch* never gets in the river, it's been fun. A great project. A great dream."

Maybe someday. Huck and Tom, on the river again. Moral of this tale: Don't give up on your dreams. Keep your dreams alive.

—Conway, Spring 2000.

5

The Mild Bunch Rides Again

Meanwhile, not so deep inside the minds of those two aging brothers lay the seeds of yet another Grand Trip West. Hot dawg! Can the terrific twosome do it again? Surely once was enough, if not too much.

We're talking about a repeat motorcycle trip from Arkansas to Idaho and return. Sort of like the one of two years earlier, in 1996. And why not? It's only five thousand miles and there're two weeks in which to do it. And you know kids—never satisfied. Always wanting to go outside and play some more. And besides, the motorcycles are in good shape (probably better shape than the kids) and the kids are now only sixty-five (Wally, the retired Texas lawyer) and seventy-one (myself—and now at this writing, two years later, seventy-three).

As on the previous trip, I was to travel alone on one leg of the journey. (This time the westbound leg; on the first trip it was the east- or homebound leg.) I was to meet Wally in Idaho. He was touring on his cycle (a BMW this time, rather than the now-retired Gold Wing), traveling from Houston to Boston and then to Vermont and then across Canada to Alaska and then down to Idaho. That youngster never could figure out the shortest way between two points.

I was to meet Wally at our older brother Jim's in Culdesac, Idaho. A dandy plan. We'd visit there a few days and then travel back to Arkansas together. Then Wally'd head home to Texas—if, by that time, he could remember where it was.

My outbound trip had many of the same attractions as that of two years previous. Not the least among which were visits en route with one of our sons and his family in Oklahoma and with our daughter and her husband in New Mexico. But on this trip, after those visits, I changed my route in order to see new country. As a longtime lover of the great American West, it was a delight beyond expression to tour again on those little-traveled back roads, the "blue highways" on the map. And to drink in the marvelous varieties of scenery so readily "present" when riding a motorcycle and pitching your tent at night to camp along the way.

As on the previous trip, I experienced all types of weather. North from the Four Corners (where New Mexico, Colorado, Utah, and Arizona meet) I rode in record-hot temperatures. In Utah's southeast deserts my cycle's thermometer reached 120-plus degrees. For fifty or so miles south of Moab, the wind and highway surface were so hot I released air from my expanding tires, lest, I feared, they explode.

The very next day, meandering toward Wyoming while climbing through Utah's High Uintas Wilderness Area, in the Wasatch Mountains, I rode through sleet in temperatures barely above freezing (not counting the wind chill factor on a motorcycle). I passed deep snow banks left over from the previous winter. Land of contrasts, as the travel books say.

How to single out experiences and impressions to report in so brief a space? I'll try only two.

Shortly after entering Wyoming's far southwest corner, my route took me on a lonely but beautiful winding stretch through high-valley grasslands. Rounding a corner, I sighted, about one hundred yards ahead, a solitary figure standing by an old pickup truck, waving a tattered red flag, signaling me to stop. "Watch out for the sheep ahead. And you might want to take it pretty slow," he said, in what to me sounded like an unusual accent. I noted his rather strange dress and appearance—leather breeches, almost European-looking vest, a beret setting off his deeply lined, weathered face. A Native American, I wondered? No, that wasn't quite it.

Rounding the next turn in the narrow one-lane highway, I saw them. The sheep. And not just a few sheep. Hundreds of sheep. Thousands of sheep. All headed straight for me, right down the middle of that remote narrow road, which was bordered by fences on each side. About one hundred feet of grassy shoulder to the right and to the left. Several shepherds. Some on horseback. The same unusual look. Then it dawned on me: These were Basque shepherds! From the Basque region in Spain. Later, at my Idaho brother's home, I was to learn that, yes, there were several rather large groups of Basque shepherds in this region of the West.

To shorten the story, my journey through that flock of sheep continued for mile after mile. (Thankfully the mass of sheep parted just before I plowed through them, much like the Red Sea did for Moses, though it's rather bold of me to suggest the comparison.) For what I judged to be at least five miles, and perhaps more, the sheep continued to appear around every turn of the road, filling the worn asphalt lane and shoulders from fence to fence! And we're not talking your small Arkansas sheep. These were BIG sheep. Seated on my cycle, I had to look up (it seemed) to address these sheep face to face. And look them in the eyes I did, for the whole five hundred miles, all the while keeping up just enough headway to maintain balance.

Now, use your imagination: With every additional mile the highway under my two tires became rather slick. Perhaps you can figure out why. I'll give you a hint: Sheep stuff is slicker than you think it is. And especially if you're trying to drive through it, ever so slowly, on a terribly overloaded two-wheeled vehicle and are handicapped by an inherited reluctance to speak aloud the kinds of words you're thinking.

To this day, counting sheep, rather than making me sleepy, keeps me wide awake.

A second memory. Another day, some twenty miles north of Salmon, Idaho. Headed for the Montana border. Midmorning. Rounding a curve, I noticed, some half-dozen miles ahead, a cloud of dust rise between the steep mountainsides that bordered this lovely valley. Road construction, I thought—or else there's been a landslide.

A landslide it was. Within a few minutes I came upon it, just a couple of vehicles ahead of me, one of which happened to be a county road crew. Just as I pulled off to park beside the road, the slide broke loose again, sending tons of rock across the narrow highway just a hundred yards ahead of our little group. After a quarter of an hour or so, when it seemed the worst was over and no other slides appeared imminent, the dozen of us started moving debris off the highway, boulder by bolder, rock by rock. After about a half hour we had cleared a path wide enough for at least my cycle to get through. The rest—huge boulders—would have to await the arrival of heavy equipment.

Get through I did, probably the only vehicle for hours to continue its journey. The escape enabled me to complete, on that day, my 525-mile run to my brother's home in Idaho and to repeat our grand reunion of we three brothers.

My route the last half of that day took me through Lewis and Clark country—over the fabled Lost Trail Pass on the Montana border, north to Lolo Pass, and west through country where, were it not for the help of Nez Percé Indians, the Lewis and Clark expedition would not have survived the rigors of winter. Their historic venture would have met a tragic end.

On this six-day passage I experienced what is perhaps the most valuable blessing of motorcycle touring: The gift of living in the present. In the moment. It's a gift not readily given in this life. A gift sought by the world's great religions. A gift to be totally enjoyed. A gift to remember. Always.

—Conway, Fall 2000.

6

Fifty Years and Counting

You didn't ask to hear about our fiftieth wedding anniversary, but you're going to—that is if you keep on reading. It happened August 13, 1999. Married fifty years ago that date, we were. When our four children asked how they could help us celebrate the occasion, we told them that rather than have the usual public reception that is held on such occasions, we'd prefer to have a reunion with all of our children and grandchildren. A real family get-together.

A great idea, they said—if we'd promise to stay together for the six months that remained before the actual date rolled around. We promised.

Almost immediately a grand idea emerged: Since several in our family had never seen the great American West, why not meet at our daughter and son-in-law's ranch home in New Mexico! A great idea indeed. Since Susie and Mike had recently purchased their sprawling fifteen-acre ranch complete with an almost century-old restored home, it'd be a chance to see their new place, too. And give our grandchildren a chance to ride real horses on a real western ranch! How about that.

Located in the small community of Miami (population about 200) in northeastern New Mexico, the site was perfect. We'd use a nearby (eighteen miles away) bed and breakfast as our headquarters and have cookouts and horseback rides and such at Mike and Susie's, and make side trips to places like Cimarron, Taos, Eagle's Nest, Angel Fire, and so on. Also of much interest was the nearby Philmont Scout Ranch, about twenty miles or so down the road, as the horse travels.

Present were all of our four children and their spouses and five of our seven grandchildren. The two oldest weren't able to be present; one in the army, the other beginning college that week. We booked the bed and breakfast, the Casa del Gavilan (House of the Hawk), for four days, our party being the only occupants. A grand remote Spanish-style lodge (not another dwelling or ranch building in sight). Filled with Western artifacts, marvelous art objects, Western book collections, paintings, and such that alone could hold our attention for hours, if such hours had been available.

Our children: John Jr. (a business consultant) and wife, Andrea (formerly a writer and editor for a publishing firm), from Ridgewood, New Jersey, and their children, Julia (thirteen) and Marcus (nine).

Steve (high school music and band director) and wife, Kathy (a public school administrator), from Sapulpa, Oklahoma, and their children, Jennifer (college freshman) and John Thomas (U.S. Army).

Susie (a computer analyst) and husband, Mike (high school science teacher), and their four or so horses and assorted dogs and cats and critters.

Charles (opera tenor) and wife, Alex (composer), and their

children, Harrison (four), Phoebe (two), and Joshua (three months). This latter bunch got the prize for having traveled the greatest distance—from their home in London, England.

We've got pictures.

It was a marvelous reunion. Leisurely visits, side trips to nearby points of interest, viewing photo albums and slide pictures accumulated across the decades, hikes in the area, croquet games, and cookouts at the ranch (complete with guitar playing and singing by our host, Mike) and as many "s'mores" as we wanted to prepare as we sat by the campfire!

And, perhaps the most popular, horseback rides around the ranch pasture. All this and the marvelous scene spread out before us—an unobstructed view across score upon score of miles toward the west, where the grand Sangre de Christo range still showed off an occasional snow-capped peak or two. To the north and east, the rolling plains, timeworn buttes, and distant peaks on the horizon. As the sun set, I watched, through binoculars, a cowboy work cattle into a corral on the adjoining ranch a few miles away.

For Liz and me, the highlight of the celebration was having all of our children and most of our grandchildren together. It was a rare time. A grand time. A time filled with much reflection, counting of blessings, giving of thanks. A time of deep and abiding joy.

Yet another high point for us was when, on one evening around the dinner table, our children took turns telling Liz and me how much we had meant to them. There aren't words enough in this computer, nor space on these pages, for me to say how valued those expressions were to us.

Fifty years of traveling together down life's way. What a joy. What a privilege. What a treasure. Life is so good. God is so good.

Now let's tell some more family stories and have another helping of that grand Western cookin'. And then maybe some more "s'mores"?

—Conway, Fall 2000.

7

Bone Dust

They are old now, thirty-three years and more, these scraps of paper discovered while rummaging through old file folders.

These drawings. These scribblings. These scraps of paper smudged by fingerprints, coffee stains, and rough use. Scraps faded by time. Scraps long forgotten, only to be found in a folder labeled "Tree House Stuff." A folder lost among decades of what most would call junk—and perhaps truthfully so.

But now, these thirty and more years later, these scraps of paper speak—I can almost hear them—as if they were created only yesterday. And, oh, what memories they evoke.

That century-old white oak, once a proud and majestic king of its knoll on a ridge of Magazine Mountain, had lost its top. That tree which, those years ago, had begged for a tree house. How could one possibly say no?

And, so, to dream a tree house. To imagine a platform in the sky. And then to capture those imaginings, those dreams, on scraps of paper before they fly away to join all those other long-misplaced phantoms of the heart. (Where, oh where, do those vast, innumerable hosts of heart-dreams winter? Where do such treasures hide?)

And, so, from a stack of sometimes hastily and sometimes laboriously penned drawings and scribblings—throwaway jottings—the memories come rushing in.

Hands aching from long hours scraping bark off pine poles, drilling holes (with hand-held brace and bit) for bolts to fasten wooden beams together. Hands so sore that happy laborers—father, mother, young sons, and daughter—could scarcely sleep at night. The nights in the cabin long, restless, and eager for the next fifteen hours of summer sunlight. Then, to arise early, and work again to raise our platform in the sky.

Now, these many years later, as those drawings and notes— designed to help us visualize and plan our structure—are handled and perused, I can almost hear Barbra Streisand singing. *Scattered pictures; misty watercolor memories; things were oh so simple then; the way we were.*

It is, in a way, like sifting through old bones. Old dusty bones. Digging through the dead remains of a long-gone past. But yet—these bones are alive. This past is living.

With the blessing, these scraps of drawings and notes may bear witness to a grand truth: That it is a joy to build. And even to try to build. To create. To plan. To endeavor to meet challenges, to overcome problems. To be a partner in one of the Creator's grand designs—to be a builder.

If it is a joy and wonder to travel—and it is, indeed—how much more so also to build one's own conveyances, one's own vehicle for the journey. And such it was with our tree house. Or *is* with our tree house, I should say. For like all grand dreams, which do not die simply because they are no more, our tree house lives. Our platform in the sky is still very much alive in memory, alive to transport us down the decades, across the distances, toward the uncharted future. And all the while blessing our present moments.

To travel in a tree house. What a privilege. What a joy.

—Conway, Winter 2000.